Up This Hill and Down

Up This Hill and Down

Thoughts on Life
from the
Southern Appalachians

Lee Ann Woods

Bright Mountain Books, Inc.
Asheville, North Carolina

Dedication

To my family and the people of Grainger County, Tennessee,
for blessing me with the stuff that stories are made of, and
to the folks at WNCW in Spindale
for sending those stories out over the air waves,
and
to the memory of my grandpa,
Lawrence D. Smith,
storyteller extraordinaire

Bright Mountain Books, Inc.
138 Springside Road
Asheville, NC 28803

ISBN: 0-914875-33-7 Printed in the United States of America

All commentaries aired from 1996 to 2000 on Public Radio Station WNCW in Spindale, North Carolina. "Flowers for My Soul" was published in *Spirit in the Smokies* in July 1999. "Gabriel's Healing Path" was published as "Gabriel's Healing" in *Spirit in the Smokies* in September 1999. "Catching the Bus and the Cat" was published as "Early Morning Take-out" in *Chocolate for a Woman's Blessings;* Fireside Books, 2001.

Front cover photograph by Frank J. Miller

Library of Congress Cataloging-in-Publication Data

Woods, Lee Ann, date
Up this hill and down : thoughts on life from the southern Appalachians / Lee Ann Woods.
p. cm.
ISBN 0-914875-33-7 (pbk.)
1. Appalachian Region, Southern—Social life and customs—Anecdotes. 2. Mountain whites (Southern States)—Social life and customs—Anecdotes. 3. Appalachian Region, Southern—Biography—Anecdotes. 4. Mountain whites (Southern States)— Biography—Anecdotes. 5. Mountain life—Appalachian Region, Southern—Anecdotes. 6. Woods, Lee Ann, 1964- I. Title.
F217.A65 W66 2001
975.6'9—dc21

00-012103

Bright Mountain Books, Inc.
206 Riva Ridge Drive
Fairview, NC 28730

Contents

Preface

A few months after the birth of my second child, my husband came home from work one day to find me, the baby, and his two-year-old brother all in tears.

"What's wrong?" Pat asked.

"I don't know what's the matter with me," I sniffled. "I think I just need to get out of the house a little more."

Before choosing to stay home with the children, I had been a writer for the University of Virginia's Development Office and a part-time English teacher. In addition to post-partum blues, I was experiencing stay-at-home culture shock. Fortunately, Pat was sensitive to my dilemma because he had previously been a stay-at-home dad.

"Why don't you start writing again?" he asked. In a round-about way it was that question that sparked this book. Earlier that same morning I had heard a commentator on the radio, and I remember thinking *I could do that—I could write stories for the radio*.

The following day I contacted Mark Keefe at WNCW in Spindale, our eclectic public radio affiliate, and told him that I'd like to write commentary for the station. Mark conducted a brief interview over the phone. "All right," he concluded, "send us a tape of you reading one of your pieces." I acted as if coming up with a recording of one of my stories was no big deal.

A few days later, I sat down with the most professional recording device in my house: my son's Play-Skool tape recorder. I pressed the chunky yellow and green buttons, read the piece "On Death and Living" into the fat blue microphone, and mailed the tape and the manuscript to Spindale. A couple of months later, much to my surprise, Mark asked me to contribute to WNCW on a regular basis.

I was surprised, in part, because of my Southern mountain accent. I had come to believe that radio and TV personalities had to possess that middle-America nonaccent. WNCW's willingness to air the perspective of a southern mountain woman on everything from parenting to computers to growing up in the mountains to political activism, complete with my sing-songy drawl, attests, in part, to the station's commitment to diversity.

You may or may not find that these stories reflect whatever it is that "Southern mountain women" are supposed to be. That is because we are as diverse as any other group of people. Some of us are religious, some are not. Some of us are good cooks, some are not. Some of us are passionately independent, some of us feel helpless in our circumstances.

I am proud to be a Southern Appalachian woman, but to be *only* this steals something from my wholeness. My writing occurs not merely as a result of demographics, but from wings that my parents gifted me, from stories that I heard while growing up, from observing my young sons, and on and on.

This book contains pieces written during my first three years as a commentator for WNCW. In a few instances I simply couldn't say all I wanted on a topic in the allotted four minutes. If I stretched a piece over two or three episodes, it has been combined here. The essays address a broad range of topics because lots of subjects interest me. Many of the pieces aren't so much commentaries as they are stories. Stories, though, are one of the most effective ways to make a "comment."

You can hear my new pieces on WNCW on alternate Fridays. The station is on the World Wide Web at WNCW.org. Or, if you live in the listening region, you can find it at the bottom of your FM dial.

May you enjoy *Up This Hill and Down.*

Acknowledgments

Many people made this book possible:

- Gabriel and Blaise, my beautiful boys, are constant sources of inspiration and energy. They remind me to play and laugh and go lightly.
- My husband, Pat Dunn, is ever-encouraging. He is a mathematical whiz but also offers my writing a keen editorial eye. Pat also babysits, cooks, and cleans to give me more time for writing. It's one thing for a spouse to say, "I want you to be successful," but altogether different to become a partner to help create your success. Thanks, Pat.
- My mom, Barbara Smith, has cleaned our house, folded approximately 345 million pounds of our laundry, and has spread our table with good country cookin': fried fish, fried chicken, sting beans, fresh creamed corn, biscuits, homemade fruit cobblers, and sweet iced tea. No, she doesn't live with us, she actually drives here from East Tennessee to take on such tasks, her only reward being that she gets to see her grandbabies. When Mom is around, the only thing left for me to do is write.
- Papa, Doug Smith, prompted my curiosity in the written word at an early age by his poetry recitations and by encouraging me to always ask questions. He now teaches his grandchildren this thrill of discovery. He has also added excitement to a couple of my fictional stories by placing them on canvas. To see Papa painting my words is the ultimate compliment.
- My siblings, Dr. Jennie Smith, Julie Smith, and David Smith, jump up and down when a publisher wants to see my work. And when a rejection slip comes in, they don't cry with me, they stock up on shaving cream and pay the publisher a friendly little visit. Just kidding! I'm not joking, though, about their endless support and encouragement.
- My extended family—grandparents, aunts, uncles, and cousins—have given me a museum of stories. Grandpa

Lawrence D. Smith always had stories to tell, and Grandma Edith Woods Smith grinned and giggled as Grandpa shared his tales as though they were brand new to her and not the hundredth time she had heard them. My great aunts, Ruth Woods Pearson and Naomi Woods Hina, and my great-great aunt Eula Mae Harris, modeled for me the life of strong, resourceful women, and they gave me spunk.

- Thanks to everyone at Bright Mountain Books for sharpening my writing and giving permanent form to an ethereal genre. Best of all, Bright Mountain Books is a small house dedicated to publishing Southeastern regional literature, and they do it well.

It takes a village to raise a writer.

Appalachian Life and People

"I got to eat country ham and fried chicken and biscuits and cornbread, and visit with my buddy Norman before the concert tonight. If I were a star and got whisked away and surrounded with guards, I wouldn't get to do that."

—Grammy-nominated
bluegrass/gospel performer
DOYLE LAWSON
of Bristol, Tennessee

Hillbilly Woman

I grew up in a tiny one-stoplight town in the East Tennessee mountains. For years, I never thought of my heritage as being important or something of which I should be proud. It's not that I was ashamed of where I grew up, I just didn't realize my hometown was that much different from anywhere else. But after living in what I call "cities" (and most others call "towns"), I have come to realize the wealth of culture to which I was exposed when growing up. Though the public school system in my home county was and *is* lacking, the area is rich with opportunities for exploration and learning. My sisters, brother, and I—and I dare say many other mountain kids—became intelligent, resourceful, creative, persistent, and self-confident.

The house in which I grew up was surrounded by woods. I, my sisters, brother, and a boy who lived across the road from us knew those woods. We knew which creek bed to follow to the best grapevine for swinging, which "holler" had the most trees that had fallen across the stream for us to cross, which poisonous plants and snakes to avoid. We pulled up sassafras saplings and sucked on the roots for root-beer flavor. A certain plant called heart leaf we could rub briskly between our hands and extract a wonderful perfume. We picked another plant called rat's vein and boiled it in sugar water to make a tea. We constructed lean-to's from fallen tree branches and covered the tops with moss. We knew we could crack and eat the hickory nuts and walnuts that fell to the ground, but we should avoid the acorns. We did, however, gather acorn caps and use them for whistles. An acorn-cap whistle can be more shrill than any store-bought whistle I've ever heard. We would gather tadpoles, salamanders, lizards, frogs, lightning bugs, grasshoppers, ants, and June bugs, study the critters, and return them to their homes. *We became intelligent.*

The streambed held many treasures. Not only did we learn a little about geology from all the rocks, but we'd also gather rocks, take them home, and paint scenes of the woods or sunsets on them, or glue them together to make little characters. When the rock painting became dull, we'd gather at the creek and crush various hues of sandstone into powders of green, red, orange, and yellow. We'd add a little water (or spit, if the creek had run dry) and paint our faces. *We became resourceful and creative.*

Though I refused to fish, I gladly helped dig for and catch worms. Once when doing this, we found a nest of baby black snakes. My sister gleefully took one into the kitchen to show Mom who was far from gleeful at seeing the baby snake. My sister hadn't anticipated Mom's startled reaction and she dropped the snake on the linoleum floor. Mom ran out of the house with promises of no dinner until the snake had been apprehended. Trying to catch a baby snake on a linoleum floor is like trying to rid your October yard of leaves one handful at a time: You can do it, but it takes some time and patience. Fortunately, we did manage to return the snake to its home before supper. *We became persistent.*

Once while hiking with one of my sisters, we heard a commotion and looked behind us to see a herd of cattle stampeding down the path toward us. Thinking my sister to be right behind me, I hopped off the trail, hid behind a tree, and prayed. After a few seconds the cows boomed past without a glance in my direction, but I was nearly paralyzed with fear when I couldn't find my sister. "Julie, Julie!" I screamed.

"Lee Ann, up here," a raspy voice called out. I looked to find my sister a good fifteen feet up a skinny, branchless tree.

"How did you get *up there*?" I laughed, glad to see her alive and unharmed.

"I shinnied!" she announced triumphantly.

"I didn't know you could shinny," I said.

"I can now!" she shouted. *We became self-confident.*

My rural (and what many consider *deprived*) mountain setting bestowed on me traits for which others attend expensive workshops to learn. I have grown to be proud of my heritage and where I was raised. Not everyone gets to grow up in the beauty of the Southern Appalachians, and I like being different. Whenever anyone jabs me about being a hillbilly now, I quickly retort, "Yes, I am, and proud of it!"

January 1997

Eula Mae's Secret to Long Life

In the doctor's office some time ago, I discovered an article that featured people one hundred years old or older. They were asked to reveal the secrets of their longevity. One man said, "I've never had a drink a day in my life." Another man, a couple of years older than the nondrinker, revealed that his secret to a long life lay in having a highball every day at noon.

At a glance, the stark contrast of the longevity secrets of these two gentlemen is amusing. In these days of oat bran, wheat germ, pure bottled water, organic soy products, and antioxidants, it seems that merely having a particular drink each day at a specific time, or abstaining from drinks altogether is a bit, well, simplistic. Both those centenarians perhaps held a key to long life that we, in our enlightened age of preventive health and holistic techniques, sometimes overlook. The trick to longevity must be discovering what works for each of us as individuals, be it herbal teas and tofu, or country ham and biscuits with redeye gravy, or all of the above.

My great-great-aunt Eula ate exactly what she wanted, no more, no less, and she was as tiny as she was feisty. She measured about five feet tall, weighed her age, and bragged about it. "I'm ninety-eight and I weigh ninety-eight," she'd pipe. When I asked Aunt Eula once how she lived to be so old, she quipped, "I eat green beans and a Hershey's Bar ever-day of my life." And you can be sure that those beans boiled all day long in a half-pound of fatback. Surely though, chocolate and greasy green beans were not the only secrets to Aunt Eula's long life.

Maybe her longevity had something to do with exercise. Whenever my papa, being the attentive druggist that he is, would ask Aunt Eula what she did when her arthritis started acting up, she'd answer, "I go out in my garden and hoe three rows of green beans." As if to say, "Isn't that what everybody does?"

Possibly Aunt Eula's secret lay in the herbs she sprinkled in her homemade sausage which she ate nearly every day. When she fried up her scrumptious hamburger-sized sausage patties, the grease stood nearly an inch deep in her iron skillet. Still, Aunt Eula was healthy. My mom, in a motherly tone, once asked, "Now Eula, have you been to the doctor lately?"

Aunt Eula snapped back, "No, have you?!"

Indeed, Aunt Eula's longevity could be attributed to her

stubborn and mischievous streaks and her passion for play. She developed a rhyme with her name that sent shrieks of laughter through my siblings and me every time she said it. If she felt we hadn't asked what her name was enough times during a particular day, she would implore, "Ask me my name now." So we'd play along and listen delightedly as Aunt Eula, with the sparkle of a three year old in her eyes, chanted, "Eula Mae, ran away, stuck her head in a pile of hay."

Conceivably all the attention that Aunt Eula showered on my sisters and brother and me is what kept her alive and zesty for so many years. She loved creating sugar cookies with us. After we had messed up her kitchen with all the decorating, she would pop corn and pretend that each kernel was a different animal that could hop into our mouths. Once during the middle of a particularly messy and fun sugar-cookie session, Aunt Eula's old, black, rotary-dial phone dared to interrupt her. This was long before the days of Caller ID. Aunt Eula glared at the phone, jerked up the receiver, and without bothering to say hello or ask who was calling, she snapped, "Got cump-nee! Call ye back later!" and slammed the phone back on its base.

Fortunately most people overlooked Aunt Eula's eccentricities because they viewed her as a "little old lady," although she never saw herself as such. Perhaps never thinking of herself as *little* or *old* or even *lady* is what kept her so young spirited. Still, she did not exempt others from acquiring little-old-lady status. Aunt Eula once described how, just before we arrived, she had been out delivering cookies to a little old lady who lived across the street. My mom leaned over and whispered to me, "That little old lady is probably twenty years younger than Eula."

Each summer my family picnicked with Aunt Eula in Cades Cove in the Smoky Mountains. Aunt Eula fried chicken, cooked green beans, fixed potato salad, baked a three-layer chocolate cake, brought watermelon and an array of other goodies. Whenever my mom offered to bring a few items, because there were six of us and one of her, Aunt Eula blatantly refused. One year, my mom, instead of asking, went ahead and prepared a couple of dishes for the picnic, but Aunt Eula met her with a snappy, "Well, I don't eat anybody's food but my own." To be sure, she didn't touch Mom's dishes—nor did anyone else.

After dinner, when the children and adults segregated, Aunt Eula ignored the adults and hopped in the middle of us kids, eager to start a watermelon-seed spitting and flicking contest. She taught us the science of getting the most mileage out of a seed; and no matter how attentive we were to her lessons, she always seemed to win the contests. One day, beside that rocky river in the mountains, I watched Aunt Eula place a watermelon seed on her tongue just so, shape her lips in the professional seed-spitter manner, and beam the seed far past any that we kids had spit. Aunt Eula jumped up with joy, shook her tiny hands in the air, and unapologetically declared herself the winner. I realized then that green beans, Hershey Bars, sausage, and sugar cookies, a lack of highballs, an overabundance of spunk, and especially an ability to play, all gave Aunt Eula a long life.

January 1998

A Family Tradition of Fool Finding

Please forgive me if I sound too nostalgic, but I must confess that one of my most favorite American observances has come and gone—April Fools' Day. Ah, that glorious day of the year when one can enjoy nature renewing itself with green shoots on the trees and flowers of pastel popping up from the previously frigid earth, while at the same moment scan the bright horizon for unsuspecting souls to trip with the excuse of it being April Fools' Day. Yet as anyone who knows me or my family will tell you, it doesn't have to be April 1st to play a good joke on a person. There are 364 other days of the year which one can utilize for maximum tricking pleasure.

The ability to play good tricks has been in my family for at least four generations. Before the turn of the century, my great-grandpa, who opened a pharmacy in my tiny mountain hometown, prided himself on being able to fool anyone from annoying sales reps to customers who just got on his nerves. His son, my grandfather, who also became a pharmacist and took over the management of the drugstore from his father, is an undertaker as well. My grandpa always said that he could cover his mistakes in the pharmacy by going into the funeral business.

On my wedding day, it was my grandpa who masterminded the scheme to place sardines on the car's manifold and pull the spark plug wires. It's amazing that my husband went through with the wedding. We'd only been dating a couple of weeks when, at my brother's birthday party, right after he blew out the candles, I commented on how great the cake smelled. My brother stuck his nose down to sniff the cake, and—BAM—I knocked the back of his head, leaving him with a face full of frosting and a heart bent on revenge. My grandpa laughed his approval, I grinned proudly, and my husband has been on guard ever since.

My father, who surely benefitted from observing the pranks of his father, implemented one of the most long-standing jokes anyone has ever played on me. When I was growing up, my parents occasionally took us out to eat at a particular Chinese restaurant. My sisters and brother and I were fascinated with the Chinese characters adorning the bamboo paintings, so different from our alphabet. We'd ask Papa what the writing said and he'd rattle on for a couple of minutes in, for all we knew, authentic Mandarin or Cantonese. "What does it mean in English, Papa?" we'd ask.

"May you live long, healthy life," he'd say, or something that sounded like a great Chinese fortune, taking care to omit articles and add an accent to enhance his authenticity. I must have been in high school before I finally realized the only Chinese my father knows is *wonton* and *lo mein.*

Papa has handed down to *me* the fine art of trickery, and he's found himself occasionally wearing bright red fingernail polish upon awakening from a nap in the recliner at big family gatherings. I'm proud to say that I've learned well from my predecessors. There's only one problem with all this genetic trickery—*my* kids have surely inherited the ability. So now, not only must I stay alert to the connivings of Grandpa and Papa, but I've also got to really listen with my third ear and watch with my third eye because it could be that my one- and three-year-old sons are just around the corner with some fake vomit or a squirt gun. I feel sure I'll walk into a booby trap of theirs any day now. After all, it doesn't have to be April first to find a fool.

April 1997

Smelling the Wind with Wilma Dykeman

I grew up in the East Tennessee mountains and now live in the mountains of North Carolina. I love these mountains, especially the people who inhabit them. That's in part why I fell in love with *The Tall Woman*, a novel by Wilma Dykeman. Ms. Dykeman placed her characters in an environment with which I was familiar—the Southern Appalachians—without being condescending, without making them stereotypes of the ignorant, moonshine-gulping hillbilly. Dr. R. R. Turner, professor of English at Carson-Newman College once wrote that Wilma Dykeman's characters " . . . run a realistic scale of sweet to sour. But they are not made-up people. Without being historical themselves, they have historicity."

Indeed, Ms. Dykeman has chronicled the region's history and its people in her eighteen fiction and nonfiction books. Additionally, she holds three honorary doctoral degrees, is published in many major periodicals, has received numerous awards and honors, gives lectures throughout the country, serves on the boards of many fine universities and organizations, and has appeared on the "Today" show. I discovered Wilma Dykeman when I was in my teens and looked to her as an inspiration for my own writing, but I had never met her, and never imagined that I would.

Last fall, though, I did meet Wilma Dykeman at the twenty-year dedication of Pack Memorial Library in Asheville. During her speech, Ms. Dykeman, who made no pretense of attempting to conceal her natural Southern accent, emphasized the importance of public access to education and technology. She said mindfully that attitude can undermine or increase aptitude, and aptitude will help us find attitude.

Following her speech, I introduced myself and asked if she would sign my copy of *The Tall Woman*, the same book that she had signed to my grandmother years earlier. I also explained that I would like to interview her. She gladly signed my book and said she'd be pleased to grant me an interview. I asked how to get in touch with her, thinking she'd give me her booking agent's phone number. "Just call me," she invited. Then she added energetically, "Call me first thing in the morning. I get started on my day very early."

I quickly discovered that Wilma Dykeman's idea of an early start must coincide with my hitting the snooze button the *first* time. By the time she's up, out, and working on her nineteenth book, I'm probably just starting to dig into my grapefruit. My attempts to reach Ms. Dykeman by 7:00 AM proved fruitless, but I finally spoke to her one afternoon and we agreed to meet for a chat. I hung up the phone eager and elated.

I wanted to ask a hundred questions and absorb everything she said. The sun shone brightly on the midwinter morning that we met, as if spring would pop forth at any moment. Ms. Dykeman greeted me just as warmly, easing my anxiousness. Just a few moments with Wilma Dykeman revealed that she is genteel without being submissive, educated without being patronizing, and spirited, yet well-grounded and focused.

Wilma Dykeman's genuine portrayal of the people of Appalachia whom she writes had endeared her to me for years. I gather as much professionalism as possible and ask about her background. "I read a lot as a child. And my parents read," she says. "One of my great memories is of my parents reading aloud in front of our fireplace, not to me, but to each other. Everybody always assumes that I like writing because I have a father from New York. I also like writing because I have family who have been in the Asheville area since just after the Revolutionary War."

"Why your interest in Appalachian characters?" I ask.

She answers passionately, "I am not writing from the point of view of an Appalachian or an American or a woman. I'm writing from a *character's* point of view—a whole person." Lydia McQueen is the main character in Ms. Dykeman's most popular book, *The Tall Woman.* Lydia lives in the mountains during the Civil War. What makes her real, Ms. Dykeman points out, is that Lydia could have been living in Bosnia today, where people are torn apart in their own community. "I am suspicious when I'm pigeonholed as an author of women's subjects, or Appalachia, or the South," she says. Indeed, Wilma Dykeman develops her characters from the inside, then examines how outside influences shape their lives.

Ms. Dykeman extends that same consideration to people whom she encounters. In the fifties, she and her husband traveled throughout the South conducting over three hundred interviews with governors, cotton farmers, and people in churches. They went to a Ku Klux Klan meeting and were with Martin Luther King, Jr. during the bus boycotts in Montgomery. *Neither Black Nor White,* the book which resulted from those diverse interviews, won the national Sidney Hillman Award for best book of the year on world peace, race relations, or civil liberties.

Ms. Dykeman enthusiastically tells me stories of her travels and work. An hour into our conversation, Wilma Dykeman is no longer the author and I the interviewer. She seems now an aggregate of my great-aunts. We drift to the subject of children. She tells me that as a girl, she used to sit by a stream that ran by her house and write poems—an inspiration for her first book, *The French Broad.* "What worries me," she acknowledges, "is that children are so overcommitted. The human imagination needs space and time to wander. Children watch TV on Saturday mornings instead of going outside and just . . . smelling the wind."

Before wrapping up the interview, I greedily ask what advice Ms. Dykeman gives to other writers. "The only way you learn to write is like you learn to play tennis," she says. "You write. You do it."

"What about rejection letters," I blurt out. "Did you ever get any of those?"

"Oh, yes," she reveals with a smile and twinkling eyes. "You can either get sad or get mad when you get a rejection. I got mad. But, thank God, they didn't publish those earlier works!" She suggests re-reading rejected material, rewriting, then submitting again.

Following my chat with Wilma Dykeman, I feel as if I have completed a minicourse not just in writing, but philosophy, ecology, child rearing, and spirituality. I said goodbye to Ms. Dykeman a more confident parent, a more committed writer, and feeling more free to go out and "just smell the wind."

April 1999

Connie Regan-Blake, Storyteller

When storyteller Connie Regan-Blake shares a Jack tale, you just know that she and Jack have been good buddies all their lives. When she tells a ghost story, you might find yourself calling out for your mama. When she weaves a fable, she sparkles as if she is a child again, and you walk away with a life lesson.

I was captivated by Connie Regan-Blake's deep Southern voice and her animation for the first time at the National Storytelling Festival in Jonesborough, Tennessee, and have since listened to many of her award-winning recordings. When I unexpectedly met Connie at an Arts Council meeting, I asked for an interview and she gladly consented.

We sit down to chat and I notice that Connie is focused on me, ready and willing to hear my questions. Her eyes are bright, her arms open, and she is comfortable with me. I have the idea that she's this way with most everybody.

Connie tells me that she grew up hearing stories. "Words, and just talking, were very important in my family," she explains. "We never got up from the table to go watch TV or to do other things. We always sat around and talked about the day or what was happening. One meal could almost go into the next by the time we'd sit around and just talk."

Connie says that even though no one person was considered *the* storyteller in her family, her father was incredible in the way he chose words and the way they flowed from him. "Even if you didn't know the meaning of a particular word," Connie says, "you could still get a sense of it because of its juiciness or rhythm." Choosing the right word, though, is not really a conscious decision, Connie explains. "After it happens is when you realize, ah, that's a lovely turn of phrase." Connie makes circles with her thumbs and forefingers and hooks them together. I imagine a never-ending circle of stories being passed from one generation to the next, and a chain that grows bigger with each additional story.

"Did you always want to tell stories professionally?" I ask Connie.

"I started off in numbers—I loved numbers and thought I would be a mathematician," she answers. My surprised look was not lost on her. "Math is not as dissimilar as you would think," she explains. "It has rhythm, repetition, and a sense of completion which you certainly have in stories." Connie easily integrates these two concepts that I had for so long viewed as left-brain or right-brain notions divided by a thick wall.

"So what does it take to become a storyteller?" I ask.

"I think my most important and richest preparation for being a storyteller is that I've always been a good listener," Connie acknowledges. "When I do workshops we really work on listening with your whole body in a supportive kind of way." Connie clearly knows this technique. She takes in my questions and returns thoughtful, pertinent responses, blending listening and talking as easily as she combines math and stories.

Why not give storytelling a try? Turn off the TV and tell a story to someone today. It can be real or made up. You don't have to be a professional, but if you do want to weave a tale like a pro, Connie offers workshops and classes where she will find the storyteller in you. "Your body," as Connie reminded me, "knows the language of stories."

May 1999

Country Doctor T. J. Hill: Hometown Hero

A hero is a person, not necessarily of celebrity status or pop-culture fame, but perhaps a quiet champion for a community, who has positively impacted others. I have had the good fortune of knowing a community hero throughout my life. He lives in my small, mountain hometown, is sixty-seven years old, sings in an Appalachian gospel quartet, drives an old pickup truck, and loves to play (as he states it) in his apple orchard. He could be most any Southern Appalachian native, and most of you have probably never heard of him, but this man is a hero to many.

I had the opportunity to interview Dr. T. J. Hill, of Rutledge, Tennessee, a few weeks ago. His remarkable insight and wisdom in the way he practices medicine were immediately apparent to me, as was his spirit and the love he has for his practice and people. He is, to me, a living example of how modern western medicine can and should be administered.

In an era of exorbitant fees and pounds of paperwork per appointment, Dr. Hill is unique because he charges twenty dollars for an office visit, works independently in that he employs no one to help with his nursing or administrative tasks, and accepts no third-party pays. Additionally, all his record keeping is hand done, he has never taken appointments, he has never sent bills, and has never turned anyone away because of inability to pay.

"I have never, ever turned anybody down, in all my years of practice, because they couldn't pay," he recalls. "Now, I'm not bashful about asking for my money, but if a patient tells me they just don't have it, I say, 'Well, fine,' and

I don't even write down a charge." Dr. Hill admits that for those who *are* able to pay him but haven't, he doesn't hesitate to give a gentle reminder that they're getting a little behind. "That does one of two things," he says. "It'll run 'em off or they'll pay. But I'm not going to harass anyone." Additionally, Dr. Hill doesn't charge ministers or nurses or their families. He tells me that they get enough hell without having to pay a doctor's bill.

Dr. Hill can charge small fees and operate independently partly because he has adamantly refused to accept third-party pays. When I ask why, he answers that when he used to practice obstetrics, more than twenty years ago, a few of his affluent patients had insurance, but he found that if he filed insurance on them that 1) it was ninety days before he got paid, and 2) he had to fill out forms in order to get paid, which took time. He declares that he was faced with raising his fees across the board because he didn't feel it was right to charge one fee to a person without insurance and another, higher fee to a person with insurance.

Dr. Hill says, "The insurance companies were forcing me to raise my fees, which I didn't like, so I told my patients to pay me and file their own insurance. Insurance companies keep that money for ninety days," he states. "Thirty-five to fifty-five dollars for a delivery fee isn't that much, but interest on a million dollars for ninety days is considerable. Plus, the insurance companies send everything back that doesn't have every *t* crossed and every *i* dotted, and that lets them keep the money another ninety days."

There has been considerable effort by Medicare and Blue Cross to get Dr. Hill looped into their systems. A Medicare representative told the doctor several years ago that he would soon be required to file electronically. Dr. Hill retorted, "In a pig's eye. I'm not going to spend twenty thousand dollars for a system I can't work and another twenty thousand a year to hire somebody to operate it. It's foolish." The Medicare representative said that by 1993 he'd *have* to and Dr. Hill reiterated, "*No*, I will not. I'll tell my Medicare patients that I'll see them for nothin' or they can go somewhere else."

Dr. Hill pauses in the midst of his story, anticipating my next question of "What did the Medicare rep do then?"

With a mischievous, almost boyish grin, Dr. Hill responds, "That ol' boy looked at me and said, 'And you would too!' And I told him, 'You're damn right I will!'" That Medicare representative must have hung his head and walked out of that small, no-frills office in Rutledge, Tennessee, amazed with this country doctor who valued his patients and his independence so much that he didn't care whether the government reimbursed him for patients who couldn't afford his twenty-dollar office call or not.

Dr. Hill claims that for as long as he can remember, he's wanted to be a doctor—a country doctor like the ones he knew in his hometown. He pursued his goal, graduated from the University of Tennessee at Memphis in 1953 and has been serving the people of Grainger County, Tennessee, for over forty years now.

What sets Dr. Hill apart, though, is not merely that he chose the rural mountain town of his boyhood in which to practice, nor that he lives a modest life on a farm, nor even his refusal to link up with managed-care organizations, thus declining the potential for a much higher salary. It is Dr. Hill's seemingly limitless compassion for and intense focus on the people for whom he cares that distinguishes him, and these traits have endeared him to the people of Grainger County. In speaking of one of his patients, a little boy who died in an accident, Dr. Hill recalls, "I went to be with the family and I just sat and cried with them."

Dr. Hill can express genuine empathy because he attempts to understand his patients, not as a group, but as individuals. Needles, urine screenings, and blood pressure cuffs seem almost cursory—certainly not the items around which a visit is structured. "So many doctors have no idea what their patients put up with to make a living," he tells me. "I sit and talk to mine every day about what they do."

I ask if he could define an average patient or average affliction. The question itself was moot. "If a doctor ever gets to the point where there's an average malady from an average patient, that doctor probably needs to go home," Dr. Hill states. "The interesting part of medicine is people, and *every* person is different—an individual. Sometimes during a flu epidemic I have to catch myself and make myself go over each patient. Even though a patient may have flu symptoms, something might be a little different." Dr. Hill admits that in every epidemic he finds a case he could have easily misdiagnosed if he had not focused on the person as an individual.

In addition to his regular office work, when Dr. Hill first began practicing he made many house calls, especially for childbirth. He quit practicing obstetrics because he could not afford the malpractice insurance and because he admits to having a pain every time the laboring woman had a pain. "You need a long, strong cigar and lots of patience to be an obstetrician. I didn't have either," he admits.

Even so, Dr. Hill made numerous house calls for crying babies. He says that many people didn't have vehicles or couldn't buy gasoline when he first began his practice. "Almost exactly three days after the delivery of a first baby," he relates, "I'd get a call and the parents would say, 'Doc, there's something wrong with this baby. It's cried all afternoon.' When I'd pull up in their driveway, I could hear the baby howling. I'd go in, put the baby on my shoulder, and it'd go right off to sleep. It wasn't anything in the world except that a baby knows as soon as you touch it if you're upset. And the more upset its parents got, the more it'd cry. I'd sit down and talk to the parents and tell them that there was nothing wrong with the baby, but that *they* needed to settle down." I comment to Dr. Hill that the way he calms babies and listens to his patients talk about their work could be termed *holistic medicine*. He modestly replies, "I've just always thought surgery was a rather crude way to solve a problem."

"Do you have any advice for med school graduates who are preparing to enter the profession?" I ask him.

Dr. Hill responds passionately and without hesitation, "Love your people." Then he repeats himself as if those three words are his mantra, "Love your people." After a pause he adds, "Of course there are six figures to be made in medicine. But most people develop a lifestyle and spend about what they make. What you don't spend or give away, you won't be able to use, so what difference does it make what you make?" he proposes.

Dr. Hill's philosophy of medicine purports that physicians have large egos. "If they don't," he says, "they're not worth a dime. But they should control that ego. Each time I get to thinking rather highly of myself, I think about the greatness of God and what constitutes life and death." He pauses reflectively and then reiterates, "If you don't believe in yourself, you can't expect anybody else to believe in you." It's that belief in himself that keeps Dr. Hill working and will determine when the sixty-seven year old will retire. "If I recognize that my confidence begins to go, I'll quit," he admits. "I'll go home and play in my apple orchard."

This keen sensitivity has surely brought Dr. Hill distress at the direction he sees medicine going. Insurance is adversely affecting health care in this country, he points out. "Medical insurance itself is not an evil but has been made an evil by the insurance *companies,*" he says. "Those companies are the major cause of the price of medicine being so high. In most any doctor's office except mine, you'll find an average of five employees per physician. That doctor must make five salaries every day to pay for the computers and computer operators, the insurance clerks, the business manager, and the secretary. One of my friends, a CPA, told me that he works with a group of nine doctors who have forty-seven employees."

Dr. Hill indicates that insurance conglomerates, which don't know anything about patients as distinct individuals or their situations, are pricing remedies and determining what will and will not be paid for, not doctors. "Medicine lost something when finances were turned over to a business office," he remarks. "Some of my friends who are physicians tell me that they don't even know the cost of an office call in their own office. Medicine is suffering because we're losing the art of looking at each patient as an individual and knowing what they're worth. Before long, you may be able to put your symptoms into a computer and your diagnosis will come out," he sadly predicts.

"Do you think the system will eventually break down on itself and we'll get back to practicing medicine the way you do?" I query hopefully.

Dr. Hill answers matter-of-factly, "I don't see that happening. The type of medicine I practice and the attitude I have are the medicine and attitude of the physicians of my day and time. We were taught this independence in school. But many of my group have quit. I think I'm a dinosaur and my methods will become extinct. I'd like to see someone take over my practice, but I don't think it will happen with the intention of doing as I do. Several young doctors have expressed an interest—and almost an envy—in practicing the way I do but have said that they just can't."

Even though Dr. Hill doubts that anyone will continue in his footsteps and doubts that health care *will* reform, he believes that most of the things we worry about are in vain. One of his favorite quotations is: "I'm an old man and have seen many troubles, most of which have never happened." Dr. Hill keeps those troubles at bay by watching things grow, sitting in pastures and listening to cows pick grass, singing in a gospel quartet, and participating in his church. Dr. Hill also keeps his perspective by seldom taking to heart what others say about him. "Don't ever worry about what people say about you," he advises. "Half the people won't hear it, half the people who do hear it won't believe it, and the other half won't give a damn."

Dr. T. J. Hill of Rutledge, Tennessee, has cared passionately and thoroughly for his patients, learning about their lives and what makes them tick. He has lived simply on his farm with his wife who he says has been the one most positive influence in his life. He has stood up for the people whom he serves to the bureaucracies of insurance companies and government entities. Toward the end of our interview I think I've got Dr. Hill pegged, and I remark that he's quite a rebel. "I don't feel like a rebel," he gently resists, "I just feel normal. I think *all* doctors ought to feel this way."

May and June 1997

Cookbook Cookin'

Prior to getting married, I owned a few clipped and crinkle-cornered recipes that were used as bookmarks and tossed here and there. When I announced my engagement, my Aunt Bunny, a former home economist, grabbed the chance to make the most of my minuscule domestic side, and she started a Southern-bred family cookbook as a wedding gift. She distributed blank pages from a make-your-own cookbook to my fiancé's family and my family, asking for their best recipes. The collection has evolved into a sort of character history of kinfolk—surely providing as much information as family trees scribbled inside old Bibles. One of my husband's aunts even wrote, on recipe cards, an embellished family tree for the cookbook.

That same aunt included a recipe for popcorn stuffing that instructs me to combine unpopped popcorn with a few other ingredients and place into the turkey. I'm then to " . . . roast turkey five hours, or until popcorn blows the rear end off the bird."

My grandpa's contribution, "Stump Cooking," originated when Grandpa had to cut down a tree and resolved to make the most of removing the stump. His recipe: "Cut down large tree two feet from ground. Hollow out hole in center, at least two feet in diameter. Build fire with wood chips and briquettes. Get an old Electrolux and reverse hose, attach three-quarter-inch galvanized pipe to exhaust hose and blow on fire. When coals are red hot, place enough steaks on appropriate grill for enough time, for all guests' tastes, raw or well-done."

For several summers, aunts, uncles, and cousins all

gathered around the tree stump in Grandma and Grandpa's yard for "stump cookin's."

Grandma's entries in the cookbook amuse me with titles such as "Easy Cup Cakes," "One Minute Icing," and "Speedy Peach Pie." Though my grandma is a good cook, I never saw her do anything in the kitchen (or anywhere else) that took only one minute or was speedy or very easy. Easy cupcakes to me is dumping cake mix in a bowl, adding the liquid stuff, and baking. You can bet that Grandma's "Easy Cup Cakes" do not involve a store-bought mix.

Aunt Bunny, who organized the cookbook, includes a tantalizing recipe for "Chicken Breasts Supreme" that instructs me to " . . . remove skin from the chicken and rub breasts, *of the chicken*, with lemon." Aunt Evy, on the other hand, wants to make sure I'm "living right" (as she puts it) with her version of "Baptist Pound Cake."

Uncle Larry, a cowboy and farmer, perhaps hoping I would relinquish my vegetarian tendencies, supplied me with two gems: "Dead Chicken Delight," and "Hamburger What-the-Hell." The meat he tosses around in a skillet will almost trick you into thinking that you can live just fine in the South without eating your vegetables. If I ever do swear off tofu, it won't be a cheeseburger in paradise I seek, it'll sure for certain be "Hamburger What-the-Hell" on the farm.

My mom determined that the number (a single digit) of recipe cards she received could in no way do justice to her culinary expertise, so she cut additional cards out of notebook paper and contributed nearly twenty entries. She included her mother's recipe for "German Chocolate Cake," a treat my mom made at least monthly—for our preacher. And she didn't forget her "Zucchini Casserole" that she fixed weekly, sometimes more, in the summers when zucchini from our garden was so plentiful that the only way we could get rid of it was to secretly leave bagfuls on our neighbors' doorsteps.

I love this cookbook, not only because it's the cream of three generations of family recipes, but also because each entry reveals a dash about the person who wrote it. If this cookbook disappeared, a precious heirloom would be lost. But knowing my relatives, they'd turn the event into a big southern-style picnic and declare, on the spot, where this family treasure was last seen—an annual Cookbook Cookin'.

May 1997

Mr. Green's Big Yellow Bus

My kindergartner is excited about school letting out for the summer. He loves school, but he works hard at it, and he's ready for a break. He's looking forward to running through the sprinkler and getting all muddy. He can't wait to start work on his lightning bug collection, and he'll be busy at the swimming pool being a diver in his mask and snorkel.

Even with all its excitement, summer is going to bring one major letdown. Mr. Green won't be dropping by our house every weekday morning and afternoon. We won't hear Mr. Green's enthusiastic, "Good morning, Gabe!" to my kindergartner at the crack of dawn. My three year old, however eager he may be, will not see Mr. Green's smile and friendly wave. Gabe's big yellow school bus will be taking a break this summer. Mr. Green, Gabe's bus driver, will too. We'll miss Mr. Green.

After Gabe climbs safely on the bus in the mornings, Mr. Green peers through the trees in our yard searching out my three year old who stands wide-eyed at the door or window, waving hopefully. The bus doesn't pull away from the curb until he and Mr. Green swap waves. When it's warm enough for opened windows, Mr. Green, who somehow early on learned my little one's name, calls out, "Hey, Blaise!" making my preschooler feel every bit as important as the big kids who pile onto the school bus.

Just recently after Mr. Green's morning departure, Blaise puffed up his chest and exclaimed, "Mommy, Mr. Green waved to me," as if the sun could now come up.

Mr. Green has helped smooth the path to kindergarten for a protective mother and an apprehensive five year old. Gabe's days always begin with a positive ring, thanks to Mr. Green. In the afternoons, Mr. Green sees Gabe off the bus with a "See you later, buddy." Gabe doesn't come running into my arms when he steps off the bus. He waits at the bottom of our driveway for Mr. Green to drop off the last of his riders at the end of our cul-de-sac, then as the bus rumbles back down our street, Gabe and Mr. Green exchange hearty good-byes. Only after this ritual do I get to scoop Gabe up.

Thanks in part to Mr. Green, Gabe got a happy start in his first year of school, and I understand that good beginnings lay the foundation for the rest of a child's education. So at the end of summer when all the lightning bugs have been gathered, all the muddy patches in the yard explored, and all the swimming done, we'll be watching hopefully for Mr. Green and his big yellow bus to take Gabe into first grade.

May 1999

~

Aunt Naomi's Sunday Afternoons

I recently spent a delightful afternoon with my great-aunt Naomi, who is in her mid-eighties. As we reminisced, she took me back to her childhood—almost half a century before I was born—and I glimpsed a fraction of her life. When the subject turned to the sternness of her father, Papa Woods, as she called him, Aunt Naomi pulled an essay from her files that she had written while a student at Maryville College. Aunt Naomi graciously gave me permission to share the essay. Here then is a colorful glance of what it was like to be Aunt Naomi as a little kid on Sunday afternoons.

SUNDAY AFTERNOON

BY NAOMI WOODS

> If I were making a list of my pet aversions I think I should place near the top my dislike for Sunday afternoon. My distaste for this particular portion of the week—which has become in my own family an institution—is the result of conditions and conflicts which are not a part of the experience of the average young person of today. The conditions were those of the traditional (now almost extinct) Puritan household. The conflicts were those which inevitably ensue when a stern and righteous parent finds himself the unfortunate possessor of a "do-as-I-please" child.
>
> It is far from my intention to criticize or belittle the sincere and loving efforts on the part of my parents to "bring up a child in the way he should go," nor do I seek to refute any of the Ten Commandments. I wish merely to establish the grounds for my initial assertion, which is made as a result of unusual experiences in methods of

Sabbath observance. Only those who have been brought up under the dispensation of what is perhaps the last generation (and some doubt that they exist even now) of strict Sabbath observers can appreciate the peculiarity of my attitude toward Sunday in general and toward Sunday afternoon in particular.

Even in my childhood, Sunday was the dread of my existence; for it was a day during which I was bound, hand and foot, by the chains of puritanical restraint. I have often thought that my father must have mis-read the Fourth Commandment—which he so rigidly and righteously attempted to enforce—into "Remember the Sabbath day to keep it *idle*", for on Sunday he attempted to suppress every form of activity except the regular attendance of church in the morning, and the meditative perusal, in the afternoon, of religious or morally instructive literature. The required church going was not objectionable to me, and on a rainy Sunday afternoon, restrictions such as my father imposed were at least endurable. When both the weather and my youthful associates were extremely inviting, the urge for outdoor activities was so great that it was almost intolerable torture for a child of my temperament to be forced to remain for the greater part of Sunday afternoon within doors, under the ever suspecting eyes of my elders, poring over the spiritual texts designed to "feed my soul."

As I became older and surprisingly (to my parents) unmanageable, I often attempted, under cover, to satisfy my weekly soul hunger with reading materials of a less formidable nature than those which were usually prescribed for me. Such attempts, however, were usually thwarted. Every magazine or book found in my hands on the afternoon of the Sabbath was subjected to the crucial test of my paternal censor. "Is that a Sunday book you are reading?" was the question invariably put to me upon its discovery. My answer, if affirmative, would be accepted only after further inquiry or inspection as to the author, the title, and the nature of the subject matter.

Or if my answer were negative, the tirade of reproof and admonition generally forthcoming served to discourage for some time struggles for Sunday reading liberties. Precious few of my chosen books escaped expurgation as worldly and unfit for Sunday perusal.

This early confinement of my Sunday afternoon's diversions to the monosyllabic monotony of *Pilgrim's Progress*, to the didacticism of the Sunday school sheets, and to the intricacies of the King James Version is without doubt the source of my unduly strong dislike for that Sunday interval of leisure which is to most persons the most enjoyable period of the week.

June 1998

~

Donald Davis, Quilter of Stories

Donald Davis is a quilter, yet I have never seen him push a needle through cotton batting. Words are his fabric, and his audiences snuggle into his handiwork. Mr. Davis is a storyteller who spins colorful tales of growing up in Haywood County, of people he knows, and more and more stories that, as he says, "just keep pouring out all the time."

Donald Davis scrunches up his eyebrows and nose as he demonstrates to his laughing listeners how very serious his high school typing teacher was about her subject matter, and how very un-serious most of her students were. Later, during the same performance, Mr. Davis's eyes grow big, and he seems to make contact with each of his listeners while he, as an adult, takes us on a nostalgic visit to his old high school which burned just recently.

Mr. Davis sews various emotions into his quilts, but there is one thread that runs throughout. That is the genuineness of his tales. He told me that he uses no script, that all his stories are orally processed. Just prior to our interview, I'd heard Mr. Davis share a tale about getting lost with a friend while hiking Mount LeConte in the snow. The audience was captivated. Mr. Davis pieced the story together so well that it seemed he had told it many times before. Yet he revealed that what I'd heard was the first telling of the story.

Mr. Davis explains his process: "I'm just quilting," he points out. "I'm picking up little scraps and putting them together, with awareness of the order in which the scraps go to make the pattern work. And you wear these pieces of cloth—they're real."

Indeed, Donald Davis has made many quilts. He's created numerous books and tapes and makes hundreds of appearances throughout the world each year. Still, he lays claim to no favorite story. "My favorite is one I haven't done yet," he says with a boyish sparkle in his eyes. "That keeps me working and looking for new things."

Donald Davis didn't start out wanting to become a storyteller. "It happened totally in reverse," he says. In Haywood County where he grew up, there wasn't anything called *storytelling*. But his family "went visiting," and the adults talked all afternoon. The young Donald would then go to school and repeat what he'd heard. Throughout the years, people would ask him to tell more and more stories. His career path led him to become a Methodist minister, but he couldn't get away from the storytelling requests.

He eventually received invitations to the National Storytelling Festival in Jonesborough, Tennessee, but turned down the summons a couple of times because, as he says, "I didn't think I was a storyteller." Finally in 1981, he performed in Jonesborough, and from that time on his life took a different path. "There was no hiding from it," he declares, "and I love it."

I, surely one of many, am pleased that Donald Davis is a quilter of stories. Otherwise, I might never have been blanketed in "Christmas in Sulfur Springs," "The Strongest Woman," "Southern Belles," "Winning and Losing," or "Otto and Marguerite"—all stories which form brilliant quilts that envelop their recipients in a little Appalachian history, a few smiles and tears, and a lot of warmth.

September 1999

Bluegrass and Gospel with Soul

I've never been a big bluegrass or gospel fan. I prefer the rhythms and expressiveness of soul, jazz, and R&B, but I've recently been turned on to Doyle Lawson & Quicksilver, an authentic bluegrass and gospel group. I find in their music some of the same traits as in the genres to which I have been loyal: spirit, spunk, and a theme of "life can be tough, but persevere." The group's songs are real, not a candy-coated dose of a generic love affair, or an attempt at tear-jerking with excerpts from the diary of an inmate whose mama got hit by a train.

Doyle Lawson, who sings and plays the mandolin, is a legend in bluegrass music—known to have single-handedly revived the nearly extinct one-mike system popular with groups in the forties and fifties. I had the pleasure of getting to speak with Doyle prior to a performance in Tennessee in

July. I found that he's a lot like the music he sings: genuine, gutsy, and unapologetic.

Doyle said that when he first started playing professional music his groups had only one microphone, and they were glad to have that. Two mics were considered a luxury, but as technology advanced and money became less of an issue, bands found it advantageous to use multiple mics and monitor speakers. The one-mic system, as well as the fluid on-stage choreography necessitated by it, quickly began to die. Doyle Lawson, though, recognized this nearly extinct art form and returned it to the forefront of bluegrass music. The one-mic technique delivers a more natural sound quality partly because the band members, not an audio engineer, control the sound. Using only one microphone also promotes an animation that audiences love. "It's more intimate that way on stage," Doyle asserts.

At the most recent Doyle Lawson and Quicksilver concert I attended, Doyle and his band were introduced, approached the single microphone, and immediately broke out in a toe-tapping "Julianne." The next song, "Back in My Baby's Arms Again," commanded the rapt attention of everyone, even a seven year old sitting near me. Yet this was no common jam session. Doyle Lawson and Quicksilver demonstrate choreography that is as engaging to the eye as their music is pleasing to the ear. "Watching people interact is infectious," Doyle admits.

Doyle certainly achieves a high level of interaction at the concert I'm attending. Though it's already late, and Doyle and his band are surely tired, the audience seems to be throwing energy at their feet. The band continues their elegant work with the microphone as though it's their best friend. When the song requires a blending of instruments and voices, band members manage to quickly yet gracefully angle fret boards up and out, supplely bend their bodies down and in, and huddle together like a flower closing its petals around the pistil. Then swiftly as the petals close, they open again as all but one band member fans back to reveal a single crisp voice or instrument.

In addition to being a Grammy finalist, Doyle Lawson has graced the cover of *Bluegrass Unlimited* magazine, is a prodigy on the mandolin (which he became interested in at four years old), and is a gifted composer/arranger and singer. Doyle's legend has taken him all over the world. He says he's frequently asked why he hasn't lost his southern accent, to which he responds, "I've never tried. I'm proud of my heritage."

Indeed, Doyle Lawson is as real as the farmers, school teachers, and bluegrass enthusiasts who turn out in droves to hear him. Doyle ended his first set saying that he wanted to "shake and howdy with ever-body." And that wasn't just talk. He stepped off the stage and immediately began "shaking and howdying" and giving out autographs to the crowd flanking him. The second set didn't begin until he'd finished talking to each person who offered a greeting. Surely he had no break to speak of.

I had seen Doyle do the same visiting at another concert, and I asked how he remains so down-to-earth and approachable. "My parents taught me to be what I am and to be the best I can be," he answered. "I have a hard time dealing with the status of the star thing. I'm aware of what I've done, but I do shy away from using the word *star*." Doyle goes on to say that he enjoys visiting with his friends and cousins at the concerts. "I got to eat country ham and fried chicken and biscuits and cornbread and visit with my buddy Norman before the concert tonight," he explains. "If I were a star and got whisked away and surrounded with guards, I wouldn't get to do that. All I ever wanted to do was play music and be an entertainer." Doyle pauses a moment then adds, "I let the people decide about the star part of it." I mention to Doyle that the people seem to have decided. Doyle just offers me a heart-felt grin.

September 1997

Dead Man's Finger

Having grown up as the granddaughter of a story-telling undertaker, I was seldom short on Halloween stories. I grew up hearing tales of funerals and bodies and dying, especially around the dinner table where most stories were shared.

Whenever anybody died in my small mountain hometown, it was my grandpa who got a call. The person calling would say, "Lawrence, so-and-so died."

My grandpa, without emotion but not coldly, would ask, "Where's the body?" (a dead person was always *the body*—never *he* or *she*). Grandpa would then announce, "There's a body up the road," and walk out the door.

One particular winter night after Grandpa had returned home from a call, my sisters and brother and I noticed that he carried a little white cardboard jewelry box—the kind they placed earrings in at the drugstore.

"What's in the box, Grandpa?" we questioned.

"Nothin' much," he yawned, trying to look bored. We begged him to reveal the contents of the box. "Are y'all sure you wanna know?" he challenged.

"*Yeah!!!*" we called in unison.

"Well," he consented, "the man in that wreck was cut up pretty bad. So I figured nobody would know if I just picked up one of his fingers and brought it home for y'all to look at."

"Oh sure, Grandpa. You wouldn't do nothin' like that." But noticing the mischievous grin covering his face we doubted our statement and asked, "Would you?" Grandpa slowly brought the box forward. We all gathered around. Cautiously he moved back the lid.

"Oh yuck! He really did pick up that man's finger," one of us gasped. We were thrilled and full of questions.

"Look how gray it is."

"Is that what color people turn when they die?"

"What if the family finds out you took it?"

"What're you gonna do with it when we're done lookin' at it?"

"Can we keep it?"

The finger, indeed grayish and bloody just below the knuckle, lay neatly on top of a piece of cotton right in the middle of the jewelry box. We moved in closer to examine it. A genuine dead man's finger! Even if fright had outweighed our curiosity, none of us would have dared move away like a scaredy-cat.

"Can we touch it, Grandpa?" somebody asked.

"I reckon so," he agreed with a grin.

Our heads closed in on the little box, and a couple of us felt the bony finger.

"O-o-o-oh, it's cool," somebody pointed out. Our circle tightened.

Jennie slowly reached in to feel it and as she did, quicker than we could blink, the finger sprang straight up and almost hooked her finger! "Grandpa, it jumped! It jumped!!!" we screamed.

Grandpa, his sly grin big as ever, moved his middle finger and thumb away from the outside of the box—so that the box seemed to be balanced on top of the knuckle of his index finger. He removed the bloody cotton, which we then noticed smelled suspiciously of ketchup. In the bottom of the box was a hole through which his own skinny index finger was inserted.

Lifting the box off his bloodied finger and turning to walk out of the room, he said dryly, "I better go give that man his finger back."

Not long after that winter night, my siblings and I realized that we were disappointed in having touched a fake detached body part. Grandpa could certainly have brought home the *real* thing in that jewelry box, we reasoned.

So on his next few calls we shamelessly tried to persuade Grandpa to collect some part or another off the body.

"And just what will y'all do with it once you have it?" he asked, knowing what havoc we would inevitably cause at school with such a thing.

"We'll keep it in a jar till we have grandkids and then pull it out on *them*," we giggled, trying to convince Grandpa that we'd one day be as clever as he.

"Well, I've got a better idea," Grandpa responded. "Why don't y'all just keep the story of the dead man's finger and pull that out on 'em someday?"

October 1997

~

The Search for the Perfect Christmas Tree

Unless you're in retail and have been seeing red and green since Halloween, you're probably about ready to put up the Christmas tree. Christmas-tree shopping for the first twenty-four years of my life involved pulling on hiking boots, bundling up, and heading off for the woods with my parents, sisters, brother, and often a friend or two. We'd all cram into the front of Papa's pickup truck, sometimes stacking three deep to a space, and loudly sing Christmas songs as we rode. Finding some woods in which to chop down a tree was no problem, particularly since we always got a cedar tree, and most people in my hometown considered cedars big weeds and were glad to be shed of them.

Once we hit the woods, we'd split into two or three groups, search out the best trees, come back together to confer, and sometimes repeat the entire process. Finally we would all inspect the three or four trees that had been chosen as best. Papa would inevitably rule one out by saying, "Nope, that one's got a double base." Another tree might have a bare side and it would be too difficult to decide if we should place the bare side looking out the window or facing us inside. My sisters and brother and I would always pick one tree that was three times Papa's height. Being outside with the big sky overhead dwarfed even the largest cedar, and we just knew it would be able to fit in the house. Then Papa would measure the height of the tree by holding the ax vertically above his head. The tree could be as tall as the top of the ax.

Finally we would discover the perfect tree. Not only was it just the right size, but it also rated as the "prettiest tree we've ever had." We were each allowed a few whacks with the ax, but Papa always felled it. He would then cut out pieces of red heart from the interior of the trunk for us to chew. As we half-carried, half-dragged the heavy tree back to the truck, we took care to avoid the cow pies. The spicy-sweet aroma of even the largest cedar tree can easily be dampened by cow-pie-coated branches.

It's been difficult for me to let go of the Christmas-tree-hike tradition. The urban areas where I've lived since getting married don't present many places that are friendly to hikers with axes. For a couple of Christmases, I succumbed to *paying money* for trees at grocery stores, just as I would pay for a gallon of milk. This method seemed to steal some of the sparkle from the trees. So I was thrilled when one year I spotted a nice little cedar in the woods just off a back road near our apartment. The tree would be perfect for our small home, plus going the short distance into the woods would be similar to the traditional Christmas-tree hike, and at least I wouldn't have to relent to paying money for a chopped-down tree. Problem was, my husband Pat and I didn't have an ax or a saw and our budget didn't justify buying one. But I was determined. I asked our kind but curious landlord if we could borrow his ax and ended up telling him the whole story, complete with a description of the coveted tree and its location. Our landlord grinned, handed me the ax, and offered to pay bail so that we could be sure to be home for Christmas. With that little bit of insurance, Pat and I headed off to fetch our tree. I'm happy to say that bail was not necessary.

Since I now have children and feel that I need to set an example of not stealing things, and because I would be crushed if I couldn't be with my family at Christmas because of being incarcerated, I figure that since I have to purchase a tree, the farmers market is a pretty good place. So in keeping with one bit of tradition, last year Pat and I and our boys piled into the front of our pickup. We searched the farmers market. There were plenty of fancy blue spruces, Norway pines, and Fraser firs, but no cedars. I asked a vendor where all the cedars were. He looked as if I'd just asked for Charlie Brown's Christmas tree. "Honey, there's not any cedars *for sale* anywhere that I've seen," he said. "Most people won't have a cedar tree." Just because I'm stubborn or hopeful, we searched some more, but he was right—no cedars.

Then we came upon what I thought might just be a happy compromise—a tree with a root ball. Even though it wasn't a cedar, I was pleased to have a tree that we could plant after Christmas and drape from year to year with cranberries and popcorn. The tree saw us through a joyous Christmas, but after being in the ground a couple of months it died—just as if it had been cut. In an attempt to console myself, I reasoned that maybe the tree's death was a sign that I need to let go of a tradition that I can no longer carry on (at least not legally). I can let go of the truck ride, the hike, and chewing cedar tree heart. I can even give up having a cedar. But I will stubbornly hold on to, and pass on to my children, the thrill of the search for the perfect Christmas tree.

December 1997

Aunt Naomi's Flower

In 1988, I lived with my grandmother's sister, my great-aunt Naomi, for a few months. This relationship was not what you might think. Aunt Naomi did not need me to live with her. She was not feeble or needing care from anyone. As a matter-of-fact, Aunt Naomi drove all over Knoxville visiting friends who were sick or dependent and who needed to hear her laughter or feel her warm touch or see hope and life in the sparkle of her eyes. *I* needed to live with Aunt Naomi. I was working in Knoxville and had been in a roommate situation that didn't work out. Aunt Naomi said that I could stay with her for a while.

Almost every evening when I got home, Aunt Naomi would mix grenadine and Sprite for us to sip on while we talked about our day. We would eat suppers of pizza and fruit while we watched "Wheel of Fortune." Later in the evening I would play piano for her, or Aunt Naomi would challenge me to a game of Scrabble (which she always won).

On a springtime afternoon last April, my sons and I went walking along a greenway in Maryville, Tennessee, with Aunt Naomi who now has Parkinson's Disease. Her arms flailed, and her medication made her unsteady so that she stumbled along the trail at times. She had to concentrate to stay on the path. She walks a mile of this path every day with her sister Ruth, with whom she lives, and says that she is grateful for her assisted living arrangement, or as her great-grandson calls it, "sistered living."

As we walked underneath trees boasting new green shoots and beside the babbling creek, Aunt Naomi pointed out white, purple, and yellow pansies that randomly dotted the trail. "I can't decide if someone has planted those or if birds have dropped them there," she said. "What's your theory?"

I thought for a moment and came up with a stunning, "Gee, I dunno." We stopped to admire a bright yellow pansy that had grown from a rock crevice.

"Last year," Aunt Naomi announced, "the pansy in that very spot was a brilliant red." I was pondering how anyone could remember the spot of a specific flower from one year to the next, when Aunt Naomi began reciting Tennyson's "Flower in the Crannied Wall":

> Flower in the crannied wall,
> I pluck you out of the crannies,
> I hold you here, root and all, in my hand,
> Little flower—but if I could understand
> What you are, root and all, and all in all,
> I should know what God and man is.

I don't want Aunt Naomi to have Parkinson's. I don't like to see her arms flailing and know that her eyesight is failing. I don't like to see the side effects of her medication. I found myself wanting to pray that she be relieved of this malady that plays rude games with her body. Then I remembered something Aunt Naomi had told me about her new Sunday school class. "It's a class, not a club," she had declared with no small degree of spunk. Thinking of this, I found myself unable to pray for an end to Aunt Naomi's Parkinson's. Instead I held her arm and remembered how much bigger she is than the troubles life has given her. And I prayed for myself—that I could be like her.

November 1999

Santy in the Grocery Store

It was only a few days after Halloween that people started asking my kids if they were ready for Santa and if they had been good and what they wanted for Christmas. I wanted to explain that we were still recovering from the Halloween sugar high and that I hadn't even prepared turkey and pumpkin pies for Thanksgiving yet. How could we possibly be thinking about being good and getting stuff from Santa?

Of course this wouldn't have been a fair question to put upon those good-hearted strangers who brought up Santa Claus to my kids. Whether my kids and I, and those fine strangers, were in the grocery store, drugstore, or simply getting mail out of the mailbox, we were bombarded with tinsel, stockings, stars, and angels before the last of the witches, bats, and ghosts had disappeared from the harvest-moon sky. Amid all the red and green, grown-ups found it perfectly natural on November first to ask those under the age of ten if they had seen any reindeer prancing about.

One early November day in the check-out line of the grocery store, a man in overalls holding a couple of items stood behind my son and me. This man's sun-leathered face and callused hands revealed that he worked hard for a living—maybe a farmer or a construction worker. He struck up a friendly conversation with Blaise. "How ye doin' there, li'l buddy?" he inquired. Blaise smiled at him.

The stranger in overalls pointed at a picture of Santa plastered in a corner of the soft drink display that flanked the aisle. "Hey, who is that right there?" he wanted to know. Blaise proudly told him. Here we go, I thought, more

Christmas hype, and I've still got a jack-o'-lantern sitting on my deck.

"You been good?" the man asked. Blaise looked at me as if he weren't sure of the answer to that one.

"Oh, yes sir," I chimed in.

The man turned his attention back to Blaise. "Santy gonna bring you a pony this year?" he inquired. Blaise and the man continued with their conversation while I settled up with the cashier.

As Blaise and I pushed our full buggy toward the car, the man in overalls, carrying his small bag of groceries, approached us again. He held out a closed fist to Blaise as if it contained a secret treasure. Blaise, naturally curious, opened up one of his hands to receive the gift. A shiny quarter and dime slipped into Blaise's small tender palm from the man's large, stained fingers. Blaise's eyes sparkled as much as the coins. "That's one fine young man you have there, ma'am," the stranger said. Blaise and I thanked him as he headed for his truck.

For a split second I thought of insisting that Blaise return the money, but I quickly set that notion aside. The man's gift seemed worth much more than thirty-five cents, plus Blaise had graciously accepted it. And I needed it. I needed to be reminded that the holiday season is about more than buying things. I needed to see the spirit with which those hard-earned silver coins moved from the grown man to the child. I needed to see the gratefulness in my child's eyes for a simple gift. And I needed a little nudge that the Santy on the Coke display was indeed for real.

December 1999

Through a Mountain Mama's Eyes

"I am suspicious when I'm pigeon-holed as an author of women's subjects, or Appalachia, or the South."

—Author
WILMA DYKEMAN
of Asheville, North Carolina

School of Assassins

On November 16, 1997, I was one of about two thousand who participated in a vigil and civil rights demonstration for people tortured, raped, and murdered in Latin America. The service was held just outside the grounds of the institution responsible for training Latin American soldiers in blackmail, counterinsurgency, torture techniques, and "disappearances." You and I, as American taxpayers, annually send millions of dollars to this institution—the School of the Americas (SOA) in Fort Benning, Georgia, also known as the School of Assassins.

In September 1996, the Department of Defense was forced to release Torture Training Manuals used at the School of the Americas. The manuals confirm that the school has been instructing Latin American soldiers to intimidate and murder their own people—including priests, nuns, labor organizers, student activists, and others working for the rights of the poor.

Supporters of the SOA argue that the school teaches human rights and upholds democracy. I received a letter in September from Representative Cass Ballenger in which he states: "Since the School of the Americas began training national leaders of South and Central America, military or totalitarian regimes in that region have declined and have been replaced with democracies."

Father Roy Bourgeois, a Catholic priest and former Navy officer, founded "School of the Americas Watch," an organization lobbying for the closure of the school. He asserts that, though many Latin American countries are now ruled by "democracies," not one head of state in these countries has been democratically elected. Joseph Blair, a retired SOA instructor, claims that the human rights curriculum is a facade and that the school "is a cold war dinosaur and should be closed."

The statistics are frightening: Three out of five of those responsible for the rape and murder of the American nuns in El Salvador were trained at the SOA that same year; ten of twelve of those responsible for the El Mozote, El Salvador, massacre were SOA graduates. In El Mozote 900 people were slaughtered—nearly the entire village; 131 of them were children under twelve years old.

Other SOA alumni include some of Latin America's most notorious human rights violators such as Bolivia's Banzer; Panamanian dictator Manuel Noriega, now serving time in a U.S. prison for drug trafficking; Honduran General Alvarez Martinez, who commanded the massacres of many civilians; Guatemalan Col. Julio Roberto Alpirez, who was implicated in the murders of U.S. citizen Michael Devine and Efraín Bámaca Velásquez, the Guatemalan husband of U.S. lawyer Jennifer Harbury. In Colombia over 100 of the 246 officers cited for war crimes by a 1993 international human rights tribunal were SOA graduates.

The vigil at Fort Benning on November sixteenth marked the eighth anniversary of the assassination of six Jesuit priests, their cook and her fifteen-year-old daughter by a Salvadoran Army patrol. Nineteen of the twenty-six people responsible for their murders were graduates of the School of the Americas. Defying an Army spokesperson's warnings, six hundred people quietly marched onto the grounds of the School of the Americas led by pallbearers who carried eight coffins that were filled with petitions to close the school. The marchers lifted crosses bearing the names of victims of SOA-spawned violence. The victims included one-month-old babies. A drum cadence set the pace as a singer chanted victims' names, and participants called out *presente* following each name.

Dwight Hulse, an Asheville resident, was one of the six hundred arrested and detained for walking onto the base. Mr. Hulse said that it felt good to be part of an activity that would make a difference in the human rights abuses in Latin America. "It was a source of hope and inspiration," he said, "to see so many people from across the United States, regardless of age, participating in the demonstration." Even so, Mr. Hulse stressed that because the congressional vote is so close, now is the time for us to work the hardest, contacting our representatives to let them know that we do not want our tax dollars spent on the School of Assassins.

El Salvadoran Archbishop Oscar Romero perhaps said it best before he was gunned down and killed by School of the Americas trainees, "We who have a voice must speak for the voiceless."

January 1998

Chain Letters

My mailbox defies the laws of physics in that it seemingly contains an amount of mail more than twice its size. Lately that mail has contained sufficient chain letters to defy the laws of statistics. The other categories of mail in my box are: personal (that which is from someone I know and which I usually enjoy receiving); bills (that which I don't *want* to deal with, but must); and junk mail (that which I don't want to deal with, and don't). Chain letters do not fit neatly into any of these ranks, but they do contain annoying features of each.

I have received chain letters inviting me to send recipes, books, money, and, yes folks, even panties to lucky recipients. Some of my friends evidently feel obligated to continue the chain but want to absolve me from my responsibility. A note on the panty letter read, "I thought this sounded like fun. But I know you're busy, so if you don't have time, don't worry about it." While most chain letters are innocuous, some can get downright nasty, threatening death (by natural causes of course) within a couple of months, if I'm not inclined to participate.

Chain letters are not exactly *personal* because they are usually photocopied and sent out in bulk, but they often do come from people I know and can contain what one might consider *sensitive* information. The panty letter, for instance, asked me to write my size beside my name. All modesty aside, why would I want to shop for underwear for other people, spend a bundle on postage, and wait by the mailbox to see what kind of undies I'll get and from whom, when I can simply get my own and probably with much more pleasing results.

I nearly dismissed the bill category as not applying to chain letters at all because I am accustomed to getting directly billed for a service rendered. But my wallet yelled out, "Wait a minute!" Let's say you get a chain letter that promises the potential of *earning* hundreds within the next few weeks if only you send one dollar to five people on a list. So you do that. But to continue the chain, you must properly rank your name under those lucky few above you, make more copies at ten cents each, stuff them in envelopes at about ten cents each, and mail them at thirty-two cents each, to a faceless list of names and to some friends you've been wanting to betray for a while. Heck, I'm not even sure if that's how you handle the dad-gum things. I've figured up an approximate total of $10.20, which does not include charges for your time. Of course if you were sending items such as books or panties, the tab of both dollars and time is much steeper. But, you may say, if no one breaks the chain you'll regain your $10.20 time and again, and just think of all the little goodies you'll get. Well, if you haven't realized it by now, I'll flat out tell you: I always break the chain. I'd much rather buy my *own* underwear and books than have a friend of a friend of a friend sending me such things in the mail.

I will have to admit, however, that the recipe chain letter tempted me. It would be relatively inexpensive to produce, and one might just receive some useful cooking ideas—something I'm always on the look out for. Yet, once again I muttered a "bah-humbug" and broke the chain. Stuffing photocopied pieces of paper into envelopes has never been a forte of mine.

Perhaps the junk category best suits chain letters. They are, after all, something which I do not want to deal with, albeit the letters come from friends. Along with junk mail, chain letters usually go straight to the paper recycling box. And, as far as I can tell, blowing off chain letters has not yet caused me many brushes with the grim reaper.

Actually, chain letters have one incontestably positive characteristic: They provide a springboard of a topic for commentary. So though I whine and fuss and make fun when I receive chain letters, I'm never too far away from being unscrupulous enough to use them for my own benefit. A small thank you is thus in order to those of you who have sent me chain letters: "Thanks." But please don't pass the word around that I appreciate it.

February 1997

A Mountain Woman Looks at Ebonics

The Oakland, California, school district's recent approval of Black English as a formal language sure caused a lot of uproar. Ebonics programs have been around for a while (at least in California). It's not just something the Oakland school board dreamed up to get attention. In a school district where more than half of the students drop out before they finish high school, the Oakland board's call for change is indeed warranted. What is appalling, though, is the board's contention that, "African Language Systems are genetically based and not a dialect of English," and that Ebonics should be taught as a separate language.

One step removed from this train of thought is that Black children cannot speak properly because of genetics and therefore cannot be *expected* to excel academically in standard-English environments. This seems yet another way to marginalize an already peripheral group.

I cannot claim to know or even relate to what it's like to be Black in America, but I can tell you from my Appalachian experience that to be marginalized due to differing speech patterns is distressful. Surely that marginalization is compounded for Black Americans who must contend with racial prejudice as well. For a long time, condescension from people outside the region when they heard my accent led me to feel as if I frequently needed to defend myself and prove my intelligence, which can be an exhausting way to live.

Black children, as well as southern mountain children, should not be exempt from learning standard English.

Indeed, our cultural microcosms are part of a larger standard-speaking community. Just because children learned a different form of English at home does not mean that they should be ridiculed or thought less bright. The standard-speaking majority has too long placed upon us linguistic minorities attributes which have little or nothing to do with speech patterns, such as lack of intelligence and laziness. I do not wish my aptitude to be ascertained by the fact that I say, "I'm fixin' to go," rather than "I'm getting ready to go." In this sense, I can understand the Oakland board's ruling.

Oakland is calling out to America, "Our students aren't dumb, they just speak differently than you," and is thus desperately grasping for something to which its students can relate. In my high school's state-mandated curriculum, there was no Eudora Welty, no Wilma Dykeman, and certainly no Alice Walker. There was little literature to which I could exclaim: "Yeah, that's it! That's how I want to sound when I become a writer!" Fortunately for me, my father was and is an avid reader, and he aroused in me a curiosity about Appalachian literature (which, by the way, is not an oxymoron). I even wrote my master's thesis on why Appalachian literature should be integrated into southern mountain classrooms, but I would be offended if academicians suddenly declared my dialect "genetically based" and began offering classes in Appalachian-ese. I wasn't taught Appalachian-ese in school. I knew it because of my mountain roots, and you can't get roots from a classroom, folks.

While teaching high school, I discovered that students who know their heritage and are proud of their roots are free to learn about their classmates' backgrounds and accept diversity. That's why it's important for students to begin their studies of literature with authors who speak to them, and *then* be led gently to literature outside of their comfort zones which will challenge and cause them to view life from various angles. If students can unite in diversity, they might be able to learn from each other how to grasp what those dead-white-male writers were trying to tell us.

Ebonics, when purported to be a separate language, is a weak attempt at instilling ethnic pride. It surely ignites stereotypes and fuels division across racial lines. Linguistic and academic justice lies not in teaching students how set apart they are because of language, but in examining how the cultural heritage and intelligence of each can make the classroom and community richer.

February 1997

~

Don't Get Malled by Easter

I noticed recently that the Easter Bunny will soon be visiting a mall near me. The Easter Bunny's impending arrival bothered me, and I began to fear that I might be turning into the Easter Scrooge. After all, I have a couple of young children, and the amazement in children's eyes when they behold a giant, moving, talking, albeit fake animal is almost worth a trip to the mall. Santa visits are in our not-so-far-removed past, and I'm just not sure that I'm ready for hippity-hopping off to the mall for pictures with the Easter Bunny. We seem to merely have exchanged red and green for baby blue and chickie yellow, lights and holly for plastic eggs.

What do kids do or say when they go see the Easter Bunny? Do they request items for the Bunny to leave for them, just as they did with Santa? Or are the children just supposed to sit on the bunny's lap looking cute while

Granny snaps a picture? I'm not so sure that my kids would know what to do. Obviously, I'm not capable of instructing them in this area.

My children even surprised Santa this past December when he asked what they wanted. Gabriel answered that he wanted a dinosaur, and Blaise said, "A tractor."

Santa looked at my boys and my boys looked at Santa for an awkward moment until Santa asked, "Is that it?"

"Yes," my boys replied.

"Well, you boys have a merry Christmas," Santa said.

I guess I just don't want Easter to be another holiday about getting stuff. There's so much hope and new life that Easter and spring bring that I hate to see it packed with visits to the mall and outfitting our yards in pastel-ly plastics. Spring is an opportune time to visit a farm, nature center, or petting zoo where many animals are pregnant and where new babies will soon be frisking about. Children are enchanted with real animals, especially baby ones, and they aren't nearly as intimidated by a fluffy real bunny as by an adult human in a synthetic suit.

Likewise, some of the more traditional Easter pleasures, such as coloring boiled eggs, filling baskets with treats, and egg hunts are perhaps more enjoyable for children than a mall visit. Children can unleash their natural creativity on the eggs, satisfy sweet teeth with baskets of treats, and expend some of their boundless energy hunting eggs. Children are fine examples to us adults of nature's springtime message of rest transforming into energy.

So take a hike, notice the little chartreuse shoots popping up in the trees, smell a daffodil, and if you see him, give the Easter Bunny my regards. I'm going out to play.

March 1999

Therapeutic Touch or a Bunch of Bunk?

Imagine for a moment giving a sick child aspirin or penicillin without wiping her brow with a cold washcloth or kissing her flushed cheeks. Still yet, imagine yourself as the sick one, lying in a hospital bed being attended to by medical professionals who are adept at administering the proper drug for your malady without touching you at all and without asking how you feel. How much better do you think you or your child could get with such "care"?

I have been under the optimistic assumption for some time now that western medical facilities and health care professionals are becoming more open to incorporating alternative or holistic medicines and techniques, along with whatever drugs may be prescribed. But in April, the *Journal of the American Medical Association* published the results of a science project of a nine year old who claims that Therapeutic Touch is quackery.

According to Dorothea Juno-Johnston, a practitioner and teacher of Therapeutic Touch from Black Mountain, North Carolina, Therapeutic Touch is a scientifically based, modern adaptation of several ancient healing practices. It is based on the idea that human beings are energy in the form of a field. The human energy field extends beyond the level of the skin and the Therapeutic Touch practitioner attunes herself to that energy using the hands as sensors. The practitioner may or may not touch the person physically.

Ms. Juno-Johnston, who has studied under the founders of Therapeutic Touch, asserts that it is the person being helped who is the healer, not the practitioner. The practitioner is helping tap into the body's natural ability to heal itself.

Emily Rosa, the child who conducted the experiment which supposedly debunks Therapeutic Touch, set up a cardboard screen through which Therapeutic Touch practitioners placed their hands. Emily asked them to identify which of their hands was near one of hers. The twenty-one practitioners who participated in the experiment chose the correct hand about 44 percent of the time—less than the 50 percent chance they would have had of getting it right had they just guessed.

The project was obviously flawed in terms of methodology. Dolores Krieger, professor emeritus of nursing science at New York University and a co-founder of Therapeutic Touch, said that the study should not have been conducted by its designer and that the twenty-one subjects were too few and unrepresentative. Indeed, even basic methodology and research classes teach that the researcher's expectations will affect an experiment's outcome, and that subjects should be many and represent a broad sample of the population being studied.

I dare say that many established medical professionals and researchers have a difficult time getting published in the *Journal of the American Medical Association.* The journal's willingness to publish results of a grade-school science experiment that did not conform to common professional guidelines displays how eager the AMA is to undermine holistic treatments—a position that Ms. Juno-Johnston points out is motivated by fear.

I am not claiming that Therapeutic Touch is a cure-all or that it works for all of the people all of the time, but what does? Have you ever taken ibuprofen for a headache and discovered that it didn't help? Yet if a fourth-grade science project were conducted about the ineffectiveness of ibuprofen on twenty-one individuals, do you think that its results would be published by the AMA?

My oldest son, Gabriel, was born more than three months prematurely and came very close to dying. I am grateful for the high-tech equipment and state-of-the-art medicines he was given. But those things alone did not pull him out of the hospital. My husband and I spent innumerable hours by Gabe's bedside implementing Therapeutic Touch and massage techniques, singing to him, praying for him, and visualizing clear lungs, strong legs, and a healthy, running child. Clearly, we are not completely responsible for Gabe's recovery but neither is the respirator he was on or the steroids he was given. Gabe is proof that massage in conjunction with medicine, and warm words offered along with an IV will go a long way in helping cure patients.

Many people have experienced a sense of well-being, peace, and even healing of body, mind, or spirit following the loving touch of a concerned friend, caregiver, or relative, whether an official Therapeutic Touch practitioner or not. The American Medical Association's eagerness to discredit Therapeutic Touch based on some very inconclusive findings of a nine year old not only displays a disregard for professional scientific research procedures, but also tosses to the wind millennia of universal knowledge which ascertain that *balance* is the key to a healthy life.

May 1998

Judges for the Judged

I was raised Southern Baptist. My family attended my hometown church nearly every Sunday morning and on Sunday and Wednesday evenings. My grandpa was a permanent fixture at the church every time the doors opened, and on cold mornings he went to the church before everybody else to get the furnace going. He was Baptist to the core—chair of the deacons for years and chair of the trustees of a Baptist liberal arts college—but I never heard him utter a demeaning word about women. My grandpa was comfortable enough with his sense of self that he did not need to fall into the trap of being *head* of anyone. Yes, he and my grandmother held what we could call traditional roles. When their babies started coming, she quit her social work job to raise the children and keep house; and he ran two businesses in addition to numerous civic duties. But, as far as I could tell, their marriage was a team effort—without one person lording *rights* over the other.

In this light, the recent amendment to the Southern Baptist governing document, *The Baptist Faith and Message,* which states that wives should "submit graciously" to their husbands, astounds me. It just doesn't seem true to the fine example I observed in my Baptist grandparents and many others in my hometown. Aside from the common arguments against this new amendment such as "Ain't *nobody* gonna tell me what to do," and "Hey, this is the nineties, *nineteen-nineties* that is," the amendment raises several concerns.

Of particular interest to me is that many tend to dismiss the submit-graciously directive as ignorant and backward.

Yet I can't write off this ruling to a simplistic stereotype. Though I don't have scientific data to prove it, I dare say that Southern Baptists are no less educated than the population at large. Look at Dorothy Patterson, the graciously submitting wife of the Southern Baptist Convention president. She said at a news conference, "When it comes to submitting to my husband even when he's wrong, I just do it." She holds three earned doctorate degrees, yet in spite of all this education she lists *homemaker* as her occupation.

I would like to ask Dorothy Patterson and her husband how a submit-graciously directive can send a healthy message to young people, or all people for that matter, about how they need to conduct themselves in relationships. At a revival about twelve years ago, I heard a Southern Baptist preacher espousing the virtues of wives submitting to their husbands. The pastor said that if he were wearing something that his wife did not particularly like, she should grin and bear it. Whereas, if she appeared in something he did not care for, it was his God-given responsibility to tell her to change and her duty to obey him.

The pastor went on to say that an attitude of submissiveness in girls can lead boys to Christ. As if without females kowtowing, males are doomed—through no fault of their own—to suffer eternal damnation. Clearly, such a concept is as demeaning to males as females. I glanced at all the young people, particularly the girls, in the congregation and longed for a message of mutual respect and permission to stand their ground.

In a world where more and more people are feeling rejected and alienated by the church, this "submit graciously" amendment does not unify and forge bonds, rather it draws a distinct line in the sand that one gender may cross and the other not. Yet many people, some Southern Baptists included, find a clear message of unity and love in a feminist Jesus who turned heads because he treated prostitutes and society's outcast women as worthy of God's grace.

Fortunately, Paul's request in Ephesians for women to submit graciously to their husbands is not the only standard for women that the Bible upholds. Even the Old Testament tells us of several strong female leaders. Consider Deborah, an early heroine of Israel, whose story is recounted in the book of Judges. Deborah was a respected leader and a prophetess who held a court to which Israelites came so that she would settle their disputes. One day Deborah summons an Israeli army leader and tells him that he should mobilize his troops to defeat an imminent enemy attack. Not only does the army leader submit to Deborah, but he also begs her to accompany him into battle! Deborah consents, but she warns him that the honor of conquering the opposing army will go to a woman instead of to him. So the two of them, along with ten thousand troops, go into battle together. Sure enough, following Deborah's commands, the enemy is defeated, and Deborah becomes a heroine to the Israelites. Judges 5:7 tells us, "Israel's population dwindled, until Deborah became a mother to Israel."

The leaders of the Southern Baptist Convention have requested that their followers live by an isolated piece of scripture instead of using their own discernment to interpret the Bible as a whole. If I were to choose a single piece of scripture to guide me, it would be the story in Judges of a strong-spirited, strong-willed, and strong-bodied woman who leads her people to victory, in more ways than one.

July 1998

Collecting Collectibles

I've never been much of a collector, though I did collect stamps in high school. Stamps are small and fairly cheap; and though the albums require dusting every now and then, stamps don't get on my nerves by requiring individual cleaning attention or by consuming much shelf space, which is where the collection sits now as I don't have the inclination to keep up with it. Everything I knew about geography in my teens came from collecting stamps. While in grade school, I also had a rock collection that I kept in a drawer in my room and from which I gleaned a little geology. But one day I must have decided the drawer space was too valuable for rocks, so I set my collection free, returning each species to its home in the woods. That's about the extent of my collecting career.

My mother-in-law, on the other hand, is a professional collector. Her stash includes a Christmas village which very closely approximates downtown Asheville in quantity of buildings and variety of shops but on a smaller scale; salt-and-pepper shaker sets which are packed sardine-like into a three-by-five-foot display case; and Precious Moments figurines which have overtaken a good portion of a kitchen wall that might otherwise have been usable space. To her credit, she also has a stamp collection which she actually maintains.

My mom collects all sorts of antiques but wants me to accumulate plastic McDonald's figurines, the ones that come in Happy Meals, because, as she says, they might be "worth something" one day. She tells me that I should save all of the five that we have. Yes, five. That's not because we've lost any. That's because five is the cumulative number of Happy Meals that my kids have eaten between them. My mom swallowed nearly that many Happy Meals in one week to get mini-Beanie Babies for the boys. "You had to eat Happy Meals to get Beanie Babies?" I asked her in astonishment when she revealed her escapades to me one day.

"Well, yes," she admitted.

"Were they good?" I asked her.

She tried to sound uncomplaining. "They were fine," she said. Then she gushed as only a grandparent can, "I did it for Gabe and Blaise," she proudly claimed. So now we have a bit of a Beanie Baby collection.

But I lack my mom's forethought. When I first saw a Beanie Baby I thought it was cute (as most stuffed animals are), but I didn't buy one. Then, BOOM! It seemed that suddenly adults were scrambling to Hallmark shops to buy up Beanie Babies, and stories surfaced of "retired" Beanie Babies selling for more than fifty dollars. And there was the Tickle-Me-Elmo craze last Christmas which found adults fighting over those plush toys and some paying nearly one thousand dollars for them.

I've read of cultures in which a person's worth is determined by jewels, land, cows, and even (heaven forbid) wives. Perhaps we are growing toward a culture in which one's worth is determined by possession of a Beanie Baby or Tickle Me Elmo collection. I can see the family of the future applying for their first mortgage: "Well," they'll say to the bank officer, "we don't have any land or stocks or bonds. We don't even own any cattle or have extra wives about, but we do have a couple of Tickle Me Elmos and the entire series of retired Beanie Babies."

"Approved!" the bank officer will shout with a twinkle in her eye—hoping to get her hands on those coveted stuffed animals.

Both of my children have extensive stuffed animal collections, but Gabe's favorite is of Velveteen Rabbit caliber. Teddy is loved to a fault—balding in favorite rubbing places and coming apart at the seams. This is a status that Gabe's Beanie Babies have not yet attained and probably never will. Teddy smells like Gabe, molds perfectly around Gabe's torso, and even shares some similar features with Gabe. Most adults probably would not pay a nickel for Teddy (grandparents excepted), but if he were ever misplaced, I'd offer a handsome reward for Teddy's return—maybe as much as three or four mini-Beanie Babies from a McDonald's Happy Meal. I'd also be on my knees blessing my mom for her foresight in swallowing some hamburgers in order to feed her grandsons' growing Beanie Baby collection.

July 1997

~

The Birth of Lee Ann Woods

Asheville is full of creative sixties children who weren't actually born until the seventies or early eighties—children who have, either by their own choosing or the circumstance of being born to free-spirited parents, acquired names such as Free, Rainbow, Lightfoot, and Earth. I was in a shop downtown one day, and the owner introduced himself to me as Rob. "But you can call me Ocean," he pointed out quickly, "all my close friends call me Ocean." I didn't know whether to tell him that gee, thanks, I was flattered, or that I felt the tides pulling me out the door.

Truth be known, I'm slightly envious of Ocean and his buddies, whose names were inspired by the forces of nature or the elements or outer-space terminology. I'm having a bit of an identity crisis, you see. It's my name.

I've been looking at names lately, listening to names, playing with names. My bookshelves are filled with authors whose names roll from the tongue like the glaze on a "Hot Now" Krispy Kreme doughnut. Merely saying their names puts one in a poetic or literary frame of mind. There's William, not Billy, Wordsworth. There's Maya Angelou, born Marguerite Johnson. There's Zora Neale Hurston and Henry David Thoreau and Barbara Kingsolver and Eudora Welty—all names that conjure up fine books.

It's not that I think Lee Ann Smith is a terrible name, or that I'm ashamed of it; it's just lacking in pizzazz. Also, of course, there's author Lee Smith, who has achieved fame and quite a bit of pizzazz, with a name that's extremely similar to mine. As a matter of fact, a woman visiting my house a few years ago spied a couple of Lee Smith books and asked if I had written them.

Since then I've begun envying women with first names such as Ashanti and Copeland and Arkansas—names that evoke mystery and faraway places—if not names that *inspire* authors of poetry, names that *write* poetry themselves. So I thought I'd give myself a snazzy first name—a name that people will remember. Maybe not an African name or a family name or a state but perhaps a tree. I like trees. I like nature. I like to hike. Why not? I thought Sassafras Smith sounded pretty good.

But before I started going over the WNCW airwaves as Sassafras Smith, I tried it out on a few people. I learned a few things in the process. First, a couple of the DJs have hearty laughs. Second, my brother and husband think Sassy Smith is more appropriate. And third, someone suggested that Snuffy Smith is more suited. So I chucked Sassafras.

Then my contemplative papa called one night. “What about Woods,” he asked.

I said it aloud, “Woods Smith, not bad.”

“No,” he corrected, “Lee Ann Woods.” Sounds good, I thought. It might just work. I thanked Papa and hung up the phone. I said the name over and over and wrote it down to see if it felt natural. Not only did Papa’s suggestion carry the imagery of trees, but as his mother’s maiden name, it also had roots.

So here’s to Grandma and her sisters, my great-aunts Naomi and Ruth. A new Woods woman is born.

For WNCW, this *has been* Lee Ann Smith, and *is now* Lee Ann Woods.

July 1999

Ending the Drought

I awoke early to what I recognized as thunder. *Good,* I thought, *this parched land will get some rain today.* It had been almost a month, the locals told me, since they’d seen any rain here. I dressed and opened the blinds. Bright sunlight filled every crevice of my small room, illuminating it without even the slight shadow of a cirrus cloud. Hmm, must’ve rained earlier, I guessed.

I stepped outside into the hot morning air and found the busy harvester ants clearing and rearranging their drenched mound of a home. Minute clumps of red clay moved out of a central opening one piece at a time, as tiny twigs disappeared into the hole. Wet, their nest appeared compact and more impenetrable than the easily blown-away sandy heap that was in its place just the day before. Then I remembered the water sprinklers. Sure enough, only the curving path of ground that lay within the sprinkler's arc appeared supple and well nourished. By contrast, the blades of grass outside the water's reach were unlucky enough to still be desiccated and crisp.

There was the booming again, and again, yet still no signs of rain. I went in for sun screen. If it wasn't going to rain, I would at least take advantage of the sun and do my writing outside in the soft shade of the magnolia. In the kitchen of the writers' residence where I was staying for the week, the other writers were discussing the bombings that awoke them. "That sound is bombs?" I questioned.

"Well, practice shelling over at Fort Bragg," they informed me. I filled my water bottle and returned outside.

Just practice bombs, I thought. No need to worry about my husband being carted off to a work camp to labor for weeks only then to be tortured and murdered; no cause for concern for shelling that would maim my young children, or kill their grandparents with whom they were staying, possibly leaving my children to survive on their own at three and five years old; no reason to fret about myself being raped by soldiers toting guns and anger in their hearts.

Blanketed by magnolia branches, I sat to write, but the tree's lush leaves and thick-sweet lemony scent could not drown the sound of the thunder, nearly constant now, coming from Fort Bragg.

July 1999

Fake Food

I recently brought home a blackberry muffin mix that I thought sounded pretty good. Pretty good, that is, until I read the fine print: "contains imitation blackberries," the package quietly claimed. What exactly is an "imitation" blackberry, I thought. I wondered not only why the manufacturer of my muffin mix would want to use imitation blackberries as opposed to the real thing, but also why I, the U.S. consumer, had bought something containing synthetic berries that are supposed to be edible. I must admit that the mix smelled great, and my kids enjoyed the muffins (imitation blackberries especially). The muffins were like candy to them, considering they normally get a whole grain or oat bran muffin. I, though, couldn't help being disconcerted by the fact that I was eating fake blackberries.

In her book, *How Do They Do That?*, Caroline Sutton explains how imitation products are made. It's quite a lengthy process that involves a research chemist, nuclear magnetic resonance, radio waves, and an oscilloscope. Finally, taste and smell comparisons to the real thing are conducted by flavorists. Sutton states: "Proponents of these flavors point out that synthetic flavors have greater stability and can withstand greater temperature changes than natural ones. They are more readily available, cheaper, and always the same in color and composition—a comfort to many modern consumers." Most of that I can believe, but why are synthetic flavors *cheaper* when it takes scientists, flavorists, and a barrage of high-tech equipment to formulate the taste that a simple, ripe, fresh-from-the-field strawberry offers?

It seems, however, that the nondiscriminating palate of the average U.S. consumer really does want the flavor enhancement that artificial ingredients provide, while operating under the pretense that the ingredients are natural. Sutton asserts that "the cheap synthetic flavors that consumers have been fed in recent years have made them so accustomed to an artificial taste that often they actually prefer it to a natural one." She cites one flavor manufacturer as saying that if a *bread* flavor were to be developed, the taste of Wonder Bread would be imitated, not homemade.

In all fairness to the kingpins of counterfeit foods, some synthetic things we put into our bodies are openly proclaimed as unnatural. Consider nondairy whipped topping. The description itself doesn't tell the consumer anything except that whatever the nonmilk contents are, they are whipped. Technically, the stuff could be whipped turnips. All we really know is that it's "nondairy," but still the word "dairy" thrown in gives the consoling impression that we may be getting the wholesome benefit of milk. After all, according to Sutton's research, nondairy probably *does* means more of a milky taste—even more so than milk itself.

At best, the term "nondairy" is vague; at worst it is a ploy to make oil and sugar and air and artificial flavors sound healthy by implying milk. After studying the ingredients list on the whipped-stuff tub, I thought that surely I could think of a more descriptive name than what the manufacturers had formulated. I came up with "Whipped oil and sugar compound with fake milk flavor." And you know, it gets better every time I eat it. After all, nothing's too good for me. My products deserve a boost with nuclear magnetic resonance, radio waves, and an oscilloscope. Lately, real cream has just tasted too . . . uh, real.

August 1998

". . . I Want to Be a Part of It— New York, New York"

I'm a born-and-bred country girl. Perhaps this is why I still approach large cities with some ambivalence. Mother-culture breathed into my young ears that big cities can be terrible places. They just aren't safe. They're dirty and full of crime and contain people of unscrupulous intent who are happy to prey on unstreetwise country folk. I, however, love to travel and am naturally the most curious about the spots I've been told I shouldn't venture into. I spent the July Fourth weekend in New York City and was reminded that people from place to place share a lot more commonalities than differences.

Sunday morning in New York, my husband and I boarded a public transit bus for a ride to the Metropolitan Museum of Art. The bus was filled with people of various races in their Sunday best on their way to church, chatting with each other as though they were mountain neighbors who shared a yard and a clothesline. The young man whom I sat beside silently read to himself from Proverbs.

On another morning shortly after leaving my friend's apartment, a man standing on a nearby street corner with several racks of dresses greeted me cheerfully in a thick African accent with a "Good morning, Beautiful!" Granted, he was a business man who realized that it didn't hurt to tell potential customers how gorgeous they are. Yet somehow he seemed genuine and truly happy. As I looked at his dresses, I noticed that many of the people who lived nearby seemed to know him, and they found the time to stop for a moment to chat. Of course, all of those shooting the breeze with him were "wonderful" or "beautiful" or "fabulous." I found a dress that I thought was great (of course, he loved it on me), and I happily paid the ten dollars he was asking. My New York friend told me that this man absolutely adored children and always offered a passing child a high five, and carefully looked out for his or her well-being.

On another day as I waited on a friend for about an hour near an entrance to Central Park, I observed a woman near the gate who was handing out fliers to people who entered the park. She offered nearly every person who entered a flyer, and though many refused, she didn't stop smiling or standing the entire time I was waiting on my friend. Close by her was a hot dog vendor who didn't have many customers, but I noticed him preparing an order. He wrapped the hot dog carefully and took it to the woman. "For you," he said.

"Oh, no thank you," the woman responded.

"But you've been standing here for hours and haven't eaten a thing," he countered. That hot dog man and my mama have a lot in common, I realized, with their compassion and their entreaties to try to get people to eat.

I must've been so caught up in the solicitude of the New Yorkers whom I had encountered that I forgot to look like a tourist. A woman with a heavy British accent approached me and asked for directions to the park's Central Stage. I never dreamed I'd think it, but I was actually complimented that the woman mistook me for a New Yorker (although she probably realized her mistake as soon as I opened my mouth).

The only person I encountered who was obnoxious was a tourist from the Southwest. On the bus on our way back to the airport, this man complained loudly and incessantly about public transportation in New York, the street maps and layout of the streets, and how because everything was so spread out that he couldn't manage to visit more than one tourist site per day. As the bus made its way through Harlem, this man told the bus driver that he wanted to get a picture of the Apollo Theater so that he could tell people back home that he'd been there. When the driver halted at a bus stop near the theater, she informed him that the Apollo was across the street. Yet without offering a thank you, this man complained that she had not stopped long enough and how did she expect him to get a picture from across the street with cars in the way and with the bus about to move and everything.

Unlike Mr. Whiny's trip, my stay in New York was delightful. I've learned that there is probably about the same percentage of unfriendly, switch-blade-toting, graffiti-writing criminals who lurk around the corners waiting to pounce on an unsuspecting tourist in New York City as there are ignorant, corncob pipe-smoking, barefooted hicks with knocked-out front teeth and outhouses in Western North Carolina. And, both places have their fair share of tourists.

August 1997

The Comfort of "The Unknown Zone"

"The Unknown Zone" was a treat for me on Friday nights when I was in high school. One of my sisters and I played in the band, and after those Friday night football games, we'd get home late, pop some corn, and plop down in front of the tube, eager to be entertained by fright. I liked

"The Unknown Zone" partly because it never sparked nightmares in me. It was far-fetched enough that my subconscious blew it off as not worth the time in my dreams. Few movies and TV shows today are so comforting in their foolishness. Themes seem to focus on horrors that really can happen to you or me.

There's a movie called *Breakdown* in which (as I have been told) a seemingly nice truck driver offers a woman a ride to a gas station after the car she and her husband are riding in breaks down. The truck driver then abducts her. Perhaps this could have at one time been written off to a screenwriter's overactive imagination, but whether or not *Breakdown* is true is moot. The situation could and very well may happen to any of us, and that scarcs thc popcorn right out of me.

The movie-izing of such horrors bothers me for two reasons. First, it has the potential to exploit the victims and/or make the crime more attractive to would-be sadists, and second, I feel powerless when I observe the suffering of a human or animal whom I cannot help, even if that suffering is a figment of Stephen King's imagination. What, after all, is there to prevent a dreamed-up horror from becoming real? There seems to be only a very vague line (if one at all) between fiction and nonfiction in scare films. Likewise many criminals, studies show, have difficulty distinguishing between fantasy and reality.

Historical and documentary movies such as *Roots, Ghandi,* and *Schindler's List* disturb me even more because they *are* based on real events. I do feel that such movies provide a valuable record of history and that they can inspire us to work more diligently toward civil liberties, but I just can't bring myself to watch them. I hate to even *think* of people being tortured and killed because they were the wrong religion or skin color. I'm thus not very likely to spend money to view such things on the silver screen. I did bring myself to watch *Dead Man Walking* and have played the murder scene of the teenage couple over and over in my head until I'm about to go crazy with asking myself how and why could such a thing happen. I'd probably have to seek intensive therapy if I ever watched *Schindler's List*.

Like the movies, the news is often almost too much for me to bear. Obviously material for horror flicks does not have to come only from the make-believe land of a screen-writer or from a time and place far removed. Several months ago, a group of teens brutally murdered three out of four members of a Swedish family living in Johnson City, Tennessee, who had stopped at a rest area on I-81. Then a few weeks ago in Asheville, there was the stabbing death of a mother and her five-year-old son, who witnessed his mother's murder before he was slain. My stomach churns to think of such things that are now not so unimaginable.

I wonder occasionally if my sanity lies in a favorite expression of my grandpa's: "When the news is full of good things that are happening, that's when you'll need to be worried, because you'll know then that the bad is so common that only the good is newsworthy." Even with the little I know about the world's injustices, I feel overwhelmed by the responsibility to better the planet somehow and wonder if to be silent and merely boycott the movies that have the potential to unsettle me a little is to passively accept the world's current state.

As much as I'd like to sometimes, I can't step back in time to those high-school nights in which my jitters were brought about by almost laughable circumstances and characters. "The Unknown Zone" called me into a realm of obviously fictitious existence and sometimes I want to go there again. It was naive and safe. Yet one of the best ways I can think of to deal with the horrors rampant in the movies and my world would be to bring myself to adopt Mother Jones' admonition to "Pray for the dead and fight like hell for the living." To truly fight for the living would, in a sense, be to enter the realms of the unknown.

August 1997

~

The Rock That Never Slides

I fuss when I encounter someone who epitomizes the proverbial *problem, not solution.* Yet alas, I've been one of those troublemakers the past two months. I'm one of those people the mayor of Newport, Tennessee, complained about in mid-July, those should-be I-40 travelers who, due to the rock slide, are coming through Newport, contributing to the horrible condition of the streets, and not even stopping in to patronize the local businesses. Not only that, but I've also been driving away the locals who regularly trade in town because they don't want to put up with the traffic jams and congestion caused by the likes of me. I'm part of the problem in a big way. And my mama is too.

I live in Asheville and my parents live about thirty miles east of Knoxville. We make the trip to the other's home at least once a month as my mama develops withdrawal symptoms when she's away from her grandbabies for more than a week at a time. But the big I-40 rock slide, though it hasn't caused a decrease in the quantity of our visits, has lessened the joy of the journey.

Like the church near me that has found a way to capitalize on the calamity, I tried for a while to find an upside to this whole rock-slide mess. The church's marquee reads:

"Jesus: The Rock that Never Slides." It then announces times of their "dynamite" services. But my optimism has proven tiresome. I examined my inner self to ascertain whether driving fifteen miles per hour along scenic mountain roads with the rear of an RV as my view and breathing diesel fumes instead of mountain air have increased my tolerance and patience. Or whether driving thirty miles per hour *under* the speed limit will make me realize more fully the beauty and lore in nature—maybe a particular wildflower that presented itself as only a blur on the roadside before. But no, I seem to be just as anxious as in prior trips to speed across the state line, leaving the tractor trailers and campers in my dust to envy the prowess and maneuverability of my little car.

Maybe, I thought one day during a trip, being forced to travel the back mountain highways, I've become more appreciative of the complex interstate system. But no, I still cringe when I notice the blown-up side of a mountain to make way for the four-lane megasystem that I, yes I, patronize. I still get frustrated when I encounter maintenance crews who seem to be consistently more intent on spreading gossip and rearranging their private parts than on spreading asphalt and rearranging unnecessary barriers so that traffic can flow freely.

This rock slide has even adversely affected my parenting ethics. I'm doing things I said I'd never do. I cram lollipops into my purse, and when my two year old and four year old begin asking me, as we creep through Hot Springs, if we're in Tennessee yet and when can they get out of their seats and why isn't the music louder, I simply stick suckers in their mouths.

In addition to helping toss Newport into the ditch and throwing quality parenting skills along the side of the road, the rock slide has made me a contributing player in what locals seem to think is the comic relief of the year. Those of us creeping through the mountain communities find ourselves viewed with curiosity, some suspicion, and perhaps a twinge of pity by natives who have set up rocking chairs to watch the passing traffic and who occasionally offer a few shakes of their heads as if to say, "Thank heavens, I'm not one of those fools in that mess."

When I finally abandon my car at my parents' house, my mom predictably scoops up the boys to dote over how much they've grown during the last two weeks and how they're talking so well and to reveal all the goodies she's found in the cookie aisle of the grocery store that are denied them at home. All that suits me, because after a morning spent pushing my kids and myself through exhaust-fumed congestion, literally tearing up the streets of Newport, blocking locals from patronizing the downtown businesses, and performing as one of the many clowns in the transient theater making its way through the mountains, I'm ready to claim a rocking chair on the deck and bask awhile in a quiet breeze. As I sit, I shake my head as I think of all the fools the likes of me, who are still sludging along in that mess across the mountain, and how maybe, just maybe, there was a reason for the rock that slid.

September 1997

On Death and Living

I didn't realize until I got to college that most people thought talking about death or dying was, at best, weird and, at worst, deranged. I grew up hearing about dead people around the dinner table. My grandpa was the undertaker in my southern mountain hometown, and he was always supplying us with new *true* stories about dead people and how they ended up that way. Okay, maybe his tales were a *bit* exaggerated, but at least he told them for the truth.

Not only did I get the impression that it is far from rude to discuss death while eating, but I also knew that to die is normal. I learned from Grandpa's wise observations that we humans can delay death, but it *will* happen eventually to each of us—death is "the great equalizer."

That's not necessarily to say that I hold my own inevitable death with unconcerned disregard. I'm not really looking forward to not being on earth—there's a lot that I love about living. I get real mortal thrills from whitewater rafting and eating a good southern-fried dinner. Can the afterlife provide comparable goods?

As children, my sisters and I were allowed to play in Grandpa's funeral home. We weren't allowed to be very noisy or rambunctious, but we freely roamed from the sanctuary to the embalming room to the casket display room picking out our favorite coffins. We were seldom scared in the funeral home. The concept of the dead arising to seek some sort of revenge, or even arising at all, was simply not a concept to us. Dead people, after all, were dead. A body was like an empty house in which no one was living. On several occasions Grandpa picked us up from school in the hearse. That was a real treat. We'd lie down on the cot in the back and take turns pretending to be the body.

Though I will tell you that I do not fear death, I do attempt to put it off: I eat healthy foods (except for those occasional bouts with fried green tomatoes), and I exercise and seek balance in most endeavors.

So why am I especially bothered by the way we humans tend to pretend that death won't engulf us, or even when it has obviously occurred, the way we pretend that it didn't happen? Perhaps it's the denial we practice and the synthetic nature we give death in this part of the world that troubles me. "He's not dead," I heard a well-meaning adult explain to a child once at a funeral, "he's just asleep." How confusing and frightening that must be to a child. Surely such a comment would adversely affect the child's sleeping habits.

Of course it doesn't help matters that we embalm and make up and dress up the corpse until she conceivably looks more real (or at least healthier) than she did when living. "Oh, she just looks so-o-o-o good," I've heard numerous times at a viewing. Preserving the body *is* a form of respect, yet, as we can only delay death and not circumvent it, so too can we only defer the inevitable decomposition.

One of my sisters who has lived and worked in Haiti for several years says that at a Haitian wake you see, feel, and smell death. No embalming chemicals are used. Wakes can last many days unless it's very hot, in which case the body decomposes faster so the wake is cut short. The deceased is laid out in a room in the family's house. Not only are little children permitted a glimpse of the body, they are also allowed to run in and out of the dead person's room. Such a custom surely helps one recognize the circle of life. Death, as well as energetic youth, is very much with the family and friends who pay respects, not quieted and covered.

My interest in death and funeral customs naturally leads to a fascination with graveyards. I find graveyards to be serene, contemplative retreats. They're seldom crowded; after all, few people take leisurely strolls through graveyards. Epitaphs tell puzzling stories of times past; many children could mean some sort of plague, whereas a score of young men may indicate a war. One can also reflect on the more pronounced gender biases of a preceding era, with women often being referred to only by first name and "wife of ___." The epitaphs can even give a humorous angle to an otherwise not-so-fun proposition. Consider the following by an unknown author:

> Here lies the body of Mike O'Day
> Who died maintaining his right of way.
> His right was clear, his will was strong,
> But he's just as dead as if he'd been wrong.

Epitaphs can encourage us to ponder the quality of our own lives, such as this selection by Robert Burns on William Muir's tombstone:

> If there's another world, he lives in bliss;
> If there is none, he made the best of this.

Most importantly though, being in a graveyard reminds me that, like it or not, I'll be there one day, too. So I vow to live a little more fully and write more diligently. When I get home I unplug the TV and call my eighty-three-year-old friend who invariably gives me a fresh perspective. Then I boil some collard greens, fry up a few pounds of okra, and book a whitewater rafting expedition. As Jimmy Buffett declares: "I'd rather die while I'm living than live while I'm dead."

October 1996

A Titanic Panic

Go ahead. Tell me I'm weird. Tell me I'm crazy. Tell me that I just can't be an apple-pie-eating and baseball-loving American. People are generally too polite to say it, but I've seen it in the faces of my fellow citizens. They label me "out there." They call me "deprived." I've even received a few sympathetic "poor dear" glances. No, this doesn't happen when I tell people that I voted for President Clinton. Twice. I don't get those looks when I confess that for entertainment in college I drove to the lake and smoked Swisher Sweets and chewed apple bubble gum. It's not because of a controversial political decision or strange leisure habits that my fellow Americans look at me as if I'm one of the Coneheads without the cone. It's because I haven't seen *Titanic.*

A few days before *Titanic* became available for rent, I visited a video store. The cashier enthusiastically asked, "Would you like to reserve your own copy of *Titanic?*"

"I don't think so," I said. His eyes grew so big with disbelief at my indifference that I thought he might need some calming down. "I'm just not interested," I offered. "I haven't even seen it yet." This comment did not console him.

"Wow, you must be one of the few people who hasn't," he gasped.

Later, in the electronics section of a large retail store, I remarked to the cashier how things seemed a bit slow. "Oh, just wait until tomorrow. I'll be putting up our *Titanic* display," she said proudly.

"Have you seen the movie?" I asked, realizing what a silly question that was.

"Oh, yes!" she bubbled, "six times."

I haven't seen *Titanic* yet because I'm a rebel. If there's something that everybody is doing I usually swing the other way. I say it's because my individuality is precious to me. My mom says it's only because I'm stubborn as a mule. Sometimes, though, I do deprive myself unnecessarily. What I mean is I'd probably enjoy *Titanic* if I could bring myself to watch it. After all, it is apparently like potato chips—you can't see just one.

Even so, I know four other people who have not seen *Titanic*, even once: my brother, my husband, and two of our friends. Actually, I probably know more than four who haven't seen *Titanic*, but it's not exactly the sort of thing that people, even close friends, reveal. I asked my brother why he hasn't seen it. "Aw, it's just too hyped. Plus I'm tired of everybody telling me that I *have* to see a three-hour movie," he groaned. "They always say, 'Oh, but it only feels like twenty minutes.' I just want them to tell that to my butt."

So if you think your hiney could not cope with *Titanic* either, here's seven excuses for you:

1. Is DiCaprio really *that* cute???

2. You already know the story line from friends, family, acquaintances, and strangers you bump into in the grocery store who have seen the movie a half-dozen times.

3. You already knew the story line anyway.

4. You already know the ending.

5. If you don't, I'll give you a hint: the ship sinks.

6. You don't have to watch the movie for the juicy parts. The video cover depicts DiCaprio looking longingly into Winslet's eyes while she holds in her lap a sketch of her nude breasts. You can just stand in K-Mart and drool on the video jackets.

7. In the three hours that it takes to watch the movie, you could get some real entertainment value by driving to the lake, smoking a few cigars, and chewing several wads of apple bubble gum.

October 1998

~

Junk Mail

My father has a friend who uses junk mail to his advantage. He gets on every mailing list he possibly can and receives so much junk that often it won't all fit in his box. His mail carrier must deliver it to his door. This man sorts out his personal mail and rolls the rest up, forming a tight log. He does this all year long and says that when winter hits, he's well stocked with fuel for his wood-burning stove.

To my father-in-law, who is a rural mail carrier, there's no such thing as junk mail. He seems to have developed a working respect for "business bulk," as he calls it. It's the stuff, he says, that pays a good portion of his salary.

I, however, haven't grown to appreciate junk mail. My personhood is insulted by letters which imply that, what with the added material possessions and social standing a new gold card would provide, my life would be a perpetual zip-a-dee-do-dah day. I usually mark such unsolicited mail with "remove from list," stuff it into its postage-paid envelope and return it to the sender. I frequently ponder all the trees that would still be standing if my mail box had a mind of its own and closed its flap on each piece of junk. The companies involved would surely give up and quit sending me stuff. Since mailboxes have not yet evolved to that level, my paper recycling box is a straight shot away.

I used to open *every* piece of mail and give it, at the very least, a cursory inspection. Now with two preschoolers, a part-time job, and a couple of volunteer endeavors, the majority of my mail hits the paper recycling box with the envelopes still perfectly glued. In the time it takes to open an envelope and sort through the contents, I reason, I could have changed a diaper. This thought was reinforced last week when I opened a letter from a credit card company and was preparing to return the contents to the sender when I spied the company president's name: Mr. Doody.

I even receive occasional letters from a matchmaking company inviting me to complete and send in a personal questionnaire. They've had a wonderful amount of success in hooking up people with similar interests, they tell me, and I could be next on their list of finding the right love. The company evidently spends much more money on postage than research, or they would know that I've been married nearly eight years. Perhaps in the matchmaking mail-order industry, a person in a current monogamous commitment is still considered a potential buyer.

Having my name, address, and phone number on my checks surely invites junk from mail-order marketing conglomerates which invariably discover such information and start haggling me. Unscrupulous company employees can also attempt to use check information to their advantage. I once received a letter from a man whom I did not know, asking me for a date. I read through all the chitchat, bewildered. Finally, at the end of the letter, he had the courtesy to admit that he was a record store cashier and had copied my address *and* telephone number from a check which I had handed him earlier in the week.

As the very wealthy do, I have considered ordering checks that reveal only my name, but I'm afraid I don't have the clout to pull that off. I could get a P.O. box, list it on my checks, and reveal it to questionable entities who request my address. But I would seldom drag myself to the post office, knowing that the most desirable mail would come to my home.

Except for checks, I try not to leave much of a trail. Still the junk mail—uh, *business bulk industry*—has a way of picking up my scent, and those dogs are hot on my trail. My paper recycling box has been filling up very quickly lately. Maybe I'll save a couple of trees in a round-about way this winter and create some homemade logs for my fireplace.

December 1996

~

Alternative Giving

The holiday season is here, and I enjoy so much about it: the crisp air, the parties, the excitement on the faces of children, the festive decorations, the spirit of giving. But I have found that my giving spirit can become a grieving spirit—grieving over what to get for whom, grieving over how much to spend, grieving over the pace of the season.

Several years ago in searching for a more peaceful way to celebrate the holidays, I came across alternative giving. Alternative giving means making a donation to a nonprofit organization in honor of someone. That person is sent a card to let him or her know how money that would otherwise have been spent on a knickknack was used to help stock a fish pond for a hungry village, or buy a pair of athletic shoes for an impoverished girl who likes nothing more than playing basketball. Alternative giving means making a lifestyle change that puts *things* lower down on your list and *people and resources* closer to the top. Consider these eight *E*'s of Alternative Giving:

Ecological: A simple card representing the alternative gift you've chosen in honor of someone consumes less resources than most store-bought objects.

Egalitarian: For a T-shirt that sells for twenty dollars, many U.S. corporations pay third-world workers just pennies. Instead of contributing to high-dollar profits, that twenty dollars placed in a scholarship fund can help send a student, in the United States or a developing nation, to school.

Economical: Alternative giving reduces the risk of spending your money on an object a person may not like and will possibly never use.

Easy: The rush of Christmas shopping is minimized, and for friends and family who live out of town, mailing a card in recognition of a gift is much simpler than packaging up "stuff."

Enabling: It provides the opportunity for our sisters and brothers who have been victims of poverty, natural disasters, or war to have a more productive lifestyle.

Educated: By giving alternatively, you're demonstrating your awareness of the needs and conditions of others.

Engaging: Those who received alternative gifts from you will often decide to give similarly to their friends and family the following year.

Energizing: You'll feel good about helping cut down on America's consumption, honoring family and friends with such thoughtful gifts, and benefitting a worthy cause or two.

I still sprinkle my alternative gifts with tangibles, but little by little I'm starting to overcome this cultural force to give and acquire stuff. One of my biggest motivators occurred a few years ago when I made a donation to a shelter for abused women in honor of my mom on Mother's Day. When my mom received an acknowledgment card from the shelter, she immediately called me. "Thanks for that wonderful gift," she said. "It made me feel so special—like I had actually done something to help a woman who needed it."

If you'd like some free information on alternative giving options, the nice folks at Alternatives for Simple Living would welcome an inquiry at their website (www.simpleliving.org)or by mail at 5312 Morningside Avenue, Sioux City, IO 51106.

Hope you have a happy, *and simple*, holiday season.

December 1998

Grandpa, Stars, and Y2K

Internet messages frequently ask if I'm Y2K compliant. In the grocery store, cutesy little signs tell me to stock up now for Y2K. I approach this with my usual degree of cautious cynicism. My cautious side is telling me that I should get the software for my computer, buy a generator, and stock up on enough canned and dried foods to feed my family for a couple of years. My cynical side is saying, "Bah humbug. January first is going to be like any other day." So how have I resolved this dilemma? I put a few extra cans of soup in the garage, brought in some firewood, and changed the way the year is listed on my computer to read four digits instead of two. It may work. It may not. We'll know tomorrow.

The Y2K scare has caused me to long for a world in which we aren't quite so dependent on computerized communications. When my husband and I were on the Indonesian island of Bali several years ago, we sought out a spot where we could experience a taste of the culture untainted by tourists such as ourselves. We went into the mountains and found a slow pace, friendly people, and a room among streams and gardens. At night everything was dark, save for the millions of stars that dotted the sky. It seemed we were on the tip of the world. There was very little electricity, no computers, and a deep sense of connection to the spiritual. I miss those Balinese nights, and when I remember them, I think maybe it wouldn't be so bad if we were less dependent on computers.

But then I think of my grandpa and how excited and curious he was about the advent of electricity, cars, flight, television, computers, digital communications—all achievements that occurred during his lifetime. I got on a plane with Grandpa when I was in the second grade. He went straight to the cockpit and talked to the pilot, asking questions about jets, fuel tanks, passenger capacity, and communications equipment. Once back in his seat, Grandpa explained to me the differences in 747s and DC-10s, and how such a heavy piece of machinery is able to stay airborne for hours at a time.

Grandpa's comprehension of technological advances wasn't merely academic. He applied a good part of what he learned. When his old Datsun wouldn't start up, he installed a toggle switch. When the heat from the fireplace in his living room wasn't getting to the back of the house, he cut out a hole in the wall and put a fan in. Grandpa loved piddling with technology even if the results weren't exactly aesthetic.

So I'm approaching this whole Y2K thing with no small amount of dichotomy. In spite of my practical self, there's enough of Grandpa in me to get me excited about being around for the year 2000 switcheroo and all the possibilities that the third millennium will hold. Having lived in the second millennium will be something to tell my grandkids about: "In my day," I'll say with big eyes, "we used computers that took up most of our desk space, we actually had to pick up a telephone to talk with somebody, and our vehicles ran on fossil fuels."

My grandkids will undoubtedly look at me as if my world had been black and white, or Technicolor at best. Certainly not a world of digital color and supersonic high-speed cable connections to every part of the globe. But then I'll tell them about their great-great-grandpa and how excited he got over the advent of the first television. And I'll tell them about those starry nights in Bali. Perhaps my grandkids will meet their third millennium world with the wonder of their great-great-grandpa and the serenity of a star-filled night.

Happy New Year, everybody.

December 1999

~

Crowd Control

Hoping to escape some of the lower-elevation heat last summer, my brother, my husband and I, along with our two children, crammed into our Honda Civic and headed toward Mount Mitchell, the 6000-plus-foot peak near the Blue Ridge Parkway. What with the crowded conditions of the car, we took a "short cut" that somehow tagged an extra thirty miles of curvy mountain road onto our journey. After an hour and a half cramped in the car, we were only too glad to hit the Mount Mitchell trail.

Pretty soon, though, Blaise began whining about how itchy he was. Sure enough, his tender white skin was fraught with a rash. Then Gabe informed us that something was biting him. My husband and brother yelled "ouch!" every other step, and I felt as if all of my exposed skin was being pricked with hundreds of little pins.

"No-see-ums!" an infested hiker called out, as he zoomed toward his car hitting at himself. By the time we reached the top of Mount Mitchell, a child had peed in his pants, which I figured was a fairly intelligent decision considering that the other option was to go in the woods and risk no-see-ums finding his privates.

"Nice view," we flatly announced upon arrival at the top as we clawed at our skin. Then we turned around, jetted down the mountain, and piled into the car; this time under the more crowded conditions caused by several hundred clinging no-see-ums and pee-soaked pants.

Hot, itchy, and gripy, we traveled south on the Blue Ridge Parkway. I wanted to lighten the atmosphere, so I chirped, "Why don't we all think of something we're thankful for?"

"Fine. You first," everyone hissed.

"Umm . . . okay, sure," I said, thinking hard. "I'm thankful that the car started."

My brother gritted his teeth. "Well I'm glad there were only a billion no-see-ums up there instead of a trillion," he moaned.

Gabe crossed his arms in front of his chest and pragmatically declared, "I'm not thankful for *anything* today!"

We were having a hard time living with each other, so after another fifteen minutes in the car, we decided to try another hike— this time at Craggy Gardens. We decided to risk the no-see-ums and do the trail. Thankfully, the no-see-ums weren't as plentiful at Craggy, but the normally spectacular view at the pinnacle was shrouded with gray clouds moving, guess where? *Toward us.* We felt the temp drop and a slight mist fall, so once again we turned quickly and made our way toward the car—about a mile.

Not fifty feet into our descent, the clouds opened up. We all ran. Then the adults stopped. We heard something that we hadn't heard all day—*laughter*. The children looked like drenched little kittens, but they had stopped to feel rain hitting their heads, catch raindrops on their tongues, and jump and dance in the puddles. In one of the best decisions of the day, the adults followed their example.

Half an hour later, we stacked back into the car—wet clothes, steamy, smelly bodies and all. But somehow the ride home wasn't very crowded at all.

January 2000

Funny Stuff

"I don't charge ministers or nurses, or their families. They get enough hell without having to pay a doctor's bill."

—Dr. T. J. Hill
of Rutledge, Tennessee

Catching the Bus . . . and the Cat

Considering it's a brand-new experience for me, I generally do a fine job of getting my kindergartner ready for the bus by the crack of dawn. On one unseasonably cold November morning, however, we were running a little behind, mainly because Gabe and his little brother had convinced me that they *needed* pancakes for breakfast. Even so, just before the bus arrived, Gabe was ready go—shoes on, vitamins taken, teeth brushed, coat and backpack on. But Blaise and I were still in our pajamas. As I was explaining to Gabe that I would bid him bye from the deck instead of walking him to the end of our driveway, the bus arrived.

I stepped out into the frosty morning in my bare feet to wave as Gabe headed toward the bus. Blaise decided that he needed to be outside, too; but when he opened the door and put his little feet into the bitter cold, my mothering instincts took hold, and I yelled at him for coming outside in bare feet and short-sleeved pajamas—in other words, for following my example. Blaise's three-year-old mind concocted a way to please himself *and* me—he put his feet inside and held the door wide open. Our cat, who is declawed in the front and not allowed outside, didn't waste any time in seizing the opportunity to escape. She darted through the door as though Garfield himself waited outside to congratulate her. Gabe saw this and, panic stricken, begged me to catch the cat. "I'll take care of it, honey," I said as calmly as I could muster. "You go on and get on the bus."

Gabe followed my directions with a worried look, so I resolved that I would catch the cat before the bus came back down our street. Barefooted and in my pajamas, I darted through some woods in our side yard after this five-pound animal who led me through a briar patch and around back of the house. She finally stopped long enough to hiss her disgust with me and I pounced on her. "Caught ya!" I yelled triumphantly, and just in time, too. The bus was heading back toward our house. I ran, clutching the cat, to the middle of our driveway and stood skimpily clad, but undefeated by the animal, in order to display her to Gabe—and fifty other amused kids and the wide-eyed bus driver. So what? I thought. I need to make sure that Gabe's mind will be free to concentrate on the more academic tasks of kindergarten and not a missing cat.

Never having been around a moving vehicle, the cat panicked when the busload of curious eyes neared our driveway and she used every bit of her intact back claws to slice up my arms and chest on her way to the ground. My wounds filled me with a fiery determination to not let her escape, so I dove toward the pavement, grabbing her tail. The cat scrambled, but I, with my own tail in the air, held fast with both hands, yanking behind her up the driveway and into the house.

I did it, I thought, once safely inside with the door closed. Now Gabe won't have to worry. A cold sweat filled my pores as I recalled the kindergarten's recent journal topic of "What I Saw on My Way to School Today." Please, God, don't let that be the topic today, I prayed.

When Gabe arrived home that afternoon he complained of his stomach hurting. I didn't ask if it was because he was chided by other kids due to his mommy's half-clothed early-morning display, or if his ache was a result of the pancakes we had for breakfast. From now on, though, Pop-Tarts sound like a pretty safe bet.

January 1999

With Good 'n' Plentys, the Money's in the Bag

The headline grabbed my attention, "Girls might find it's sad to be smart," it claimed. No, I wasn't standing in the check-out line of the grocery store glancing over the covers of the *National Inquirer* or the *Globe.* I was reading a fairly reputable newspaper. A study has shown, it continued, that depressed women often were bright and well-adjusted four year olds, and furthermore, psychologists have reported that " . . . smart, confident, agreeable girls may be at risk for growing into depressed women." The study, however, did not forget men and boys. Less-intelligent boys, it told me, tend to become depressed and hostile as they age, but smart boys become happy and successful adults. At least for the women a cure for depression has been discovered. It's called stupidity.

It was on a Monday that I discovered that smart girls grow to be depressed women. On Thursday of the same week, I read of a study conducted by a group of Scottish psychologists who found that women prefer men with feminine faces. The Scottish researchers also went so far as to theorize that, in general, women choose men who are likely to be loyal mates and good fathers to their children. Forgive the forthcoming cliché, but I just can't help myself—*Duh!*

The feminine faces and depressed women studies brought to mind some research information that I gathered while listening to a radio news program this past March. I learned that the sounds that lesbian women's ears *emit* are different from the sounds that heterosexual women's ears emit. I likewise recalled a TV news story in which a scientist revealed that, after years of painstaking objective research, he discovered that women are more sexually aroused by the smell of Good 'n' Plentys than by any other scent. I'm not kidding.

All this high-dollar research reminded me of a joke. On second thought, maybe it's not a joke. I probably read about it in the paper a couple of years ago. A scientist who is experimenting with a frog commands, "Jump, frog." The frog jumps. The scientist then cuts off one of the frog's legs and requests that the frog jump again. Again, the frog jumps. This happens with each of the frog's remaining legs until the frog has no legs. After the fourth leg is severed, the scientist commands, "Jump, frog." But the frog just sits there. The scientist says louder, "Jump, frog!" But no movement. Finally, the scientist yells, "*Jump, frog!*" But still, the frog doesn't budge. The scientist sighs, then records the findings in his journal: "Frog with no legs can't hear."

After learning of these scientific studies, I've decided to apply for a grant myself. I'd be much obliged if anyone out there could let me know what entities fund all this reputable research. On second thought, maybe my best bet would be to hope that the review board is comprised mostly of women who were intellectually challenged four year olds, and along with my grant request, pack Good 'n' Plentys in the envelope and pray that the board finds my proposal a turn-on.

January 1999

~

An Orange Ordeal

On Fiesta Bowl day, since I don't own many orange clothes, I dowsed my kids in officially licensed orange collegiate wear, compliments of my Tennessee-dwelling parents. Even so, my husband knew that I wouldn't exactly be stocked with U.T. stats, Tee Martin biographical information, or Tostitos that night, so he joined my bachelor brother at his house to whoop and holler and watch the game.

After I peeled the orange off the kids and got them in bed, I thought I, too, would get in the spirit of things so I grabbed a beer and sat down in front of the TV—all ready to yell and burp and do football-fan things that would demonstrate solidarity with my homeboys. There were lots of commercials, so I channel surfed a while then came back to the game and channel surfed some more. Slightly before half time, the beer worked its magic and I was ready for sleep. After all, I could easily find out who won the next day.

Before going to bed, I called my brother's place but there was no answer. "Oops," I said on my brother's answering machine, "I must've called before half time." A few minutes later my husband phoned back. I apologized for interrupting the game.

"Oh, not at all," he said, "you did call at half time. We were just outside making sure the truck was okay."

"Whaddaya mean?" I asked.

"Well," he explained, "when I pulled into David's driveway it was about two minutes till kickoff. I got out of the truck and it started sliding on the ice down toward the road. We were moving it when you called."

"Let me get this straight," I said tersely. "You went in the house to watch football knowing that the truck was slipping toward the road and then two hours later came out to, what, count the number of dents in it?"

"Well, yeah. What's so weird about that?" he asked. "I didn't want to miss kickoff."

"Look," I belted, "no more giving me a hard time about being in eleventh-hour labor and having to grab a tube of lipstick before going to the hospital."

"Wait a minute," my husband complained, "that's not the same thing."

"Oh yeah?" I argued.

My mom sided with my husband on the truck issue, partly because she was appalled that I would consider the remote for anything other than turning up the volume during the game. "You channel surfed *during* the *game!* How could you?" she chastised, "It's *Tennessee!*" But if I underestimated the thrill of a big orange win, my mom underestimated the enthusiasm of U.T. fans. School was canceled in Knoxville the day after the game, reportedly because of an incoming ice storm. But when ice, snow, and even rain failed to materialize, there was no small amount of speculation that school was out because of victory fever in Rocky Top.

Since there were no slick roads, my mom excitedly went searching Knoxville for championship clothing. She patronized shops with names such as Tennessee Fever and Hound Dogs that were packed with zealous fans scrambling toward anything orange-ish. Finally, admitting exhaustion, she lumbered home with T-shirts, sweatshirts, and caps. "But just seeing all that orange was so thrilling," she exclaimed, as if a herd of U.T. fans crowding into the same store was a sweet, orange-flavored elixir.

And even I, a major football cynic, must have sipped the syrup. After all, my husband's truck survived the game dent-free; I now actually own one orange shirt; and *"How 'bout them Vols"* is pretty fun to say. But what tickles me the most is that my neighbor's three year old, who knows all her colors, insists that the word for orange is "Go Vols!"

January 1999

~

Things You Would Never Know Without the Movies

I tend to view things, movies in particular, somewhat skeptically. Even though I want to be entertained while catching a flick, I also want to feel that Hollywood has gone to some pains to insert a little convincing reality into the land of make-believe. Still, I have fun finding those flaws which reveal that the silver screen world is, for the most part, one of imagination and that I'm "for real." A friend recently passed on to me a list of "Things You Would Never Know Without the Movies." I've edited the list and made a few of my own contributions. The list rates right up there with a bad comedy, but it made me laugh. Perhaps you'll laugh, too.

- It's easy for anyone to land a plane providing there is someone in the control tower to talk you down.
- When paying for a taxi, you don't need to look at your wallet as you take out a bill—just grab one at random and toss it at the driver. It will always be the exact fare.
- All beds have special L-shaped covers which reach up to the armpit level on a woman but only to waist level on the man lying beside her.

- All grocery shopping bags contain at least one stick of French bread—and carrots with green leafy tops.
- Once applied, lipstick will never rub off, even while scuba diving.
- The ventilation system of any building is the perfect hiding place. No one will ever think of looking for you in there, and you can travel to any other part of the building without difficulty.
- You're very likely to survive any battle in any war unless you make the mistake of showing someone a picture of your sweetheart back home.
- Computers never display a cursor on screen but will always read: "Enter Password Now."
- The Chief of Police will always suspend his star detective or give him forty-eight hours to finish the job.
- A detective can only solve a case once he's been suspended from duty.
- During all police investigations it will be necessary to visit a strip club at least once.
- You know when someone has hung up on you because you will hear a low steady tone. If this happens, try rapidly pressing the receiver button to bring the person back.
- All bombs are fitted with electronic timing devices with large red digital read-outs so you know exactly when they're going to explode.
- It is always possible to park directly outside the building you are visiting.
- If you're mean and you're Caucasian, it's necessary to have a German accent.
- Cars that lack bulletproof windows are equipped with peepholes under the dash. This allows the driver to duck down while being shot at and still stay on the road.
- A man will show no pain while taking the most ferocious beating but will wince when a woman tries to clean his wounds.

- It doesn't matter if you are heavily outnumbered in a fight involving martial arts—your enemies will wait patiently to attack you one by one while dancing around in a threatening manner until you have knocked out their predecessors.
- A cop or a good guy driving a 1982 Dodge Aires can usually outmaneuver a bad guy in a 1998 Porsche.

There, now you know things you would never have known without the movies.

February 1999

~

Virtual Pets

Virtual pets are the information age's answer to the pet rocks of the seventies but with one big difference—virtual pets demand attention. As with most of the inventions of the information age, virtual pets contain computer chips and therefore add to our frenetic lifestyle. You don't think the yuppie entrepreneurs of the nineties are going to invent a pet alternative that will just sit idly collecting dust do you? You don't think the consumer of the nineties will allow a manufacturer to slap two eyes on an inanimate object labeled "pet," and rush out to buy it, do you? No. We the people of the information age want to keep company with an interactive computer-chip-containing object every chance we get, and teens are following our example.

Enter virtual pets: little critters that get under my skin like chiggers. Considering that I am an animal lover, I never expected to be so resentful of a pet of any kind. Surprisingly, my collegiate dictionary came to my defense. The number one definition of *virtual* is, "being such in force or effect, though not actually or expressly such." *Virtually* is defined as "for the most part; almost wholly; just about." One could logically surmise, therefore, that virtual pets are, in fact, pets but without being "actually or expressly such." Go figure.

Virtual pets remind me of an assignment made by a teacher in my high school. Her students were to carry raw eggs around for several days. They had to take good care of them because the eggs were, virtually, their babies. An intact egg at the end of this assignment was indication that one could tackle parenthood with similar success.

Fortunately I never took that class. In spite of their virtual significance, those little eggs were, after all, little eggs. They didn't even produce baby chicks, much less a baby human. If an egg broke, it wasn't scooped up and rushed to the emergency room by a worry-sick parent. Not one egg woke its parent for a two o'clock feeding or gazed wide-eyed at its parent while cooing with contentment after a lullaby. Since then, I have learned of other schools in which the students are required to tote around bags of flour as virtual babies. At least the size and weight of a bag of flour more closely approximates a real baby.

If one wants a pet, why not get the real thing? Granted, a virtual pet won't pee on your carpet, except maybe virtually; and I much prefer virtual pee to the real thing when it's on my floor. Perhaps the birth of virtual pets has been a relief for parents whose fourth graders have bugged them since first grade about getting a cute little doggie. It was probably many a kid who got a virtual pet for Christmas. After all, most virtual pets cost less than five bucks, and, except for an occasional battery replacement, one doesn't even have to pay vet bills.

However, peer pressure excepted, I just don't understand why a kid would *want* a virtual pet. It's all the responsibility and none of the warm, wiggly, furry stuff. Also, I wonder what kind of responsibility and/or ethics virtual pets instill in our little hopes for the future. I've heard several kids pronounce, "I always kill my pet," or, "I ignore my pet and let it die." These statements, as you might guess, are not accompanied by tears of sorrow and grief for the lost virtual pet. These comments are made with pride, while at the same time attempting to convey apathy. I haven't determined if it's more cool to kill your pet on purpose or to neglect it to death. There must be an unspoken competition among junior high students to see how many virtual pets they can go through in a week. Surely the manufacturers of virtual pets would be pleased with such a contest. After all, it ain't virtual bucks that are bringing the fake pets home.

My answer to the virtual pet concept is to make the virtual part not the pet itself but the unpleasantries associated with pet care. In Utopia, you could have a *real* pet but virtual responsibilities. Real pets would come with pocket-sized virtual responsibilities computers. That way teens could experience all the love and affection of a real pet without any of the hassles.

Consider the following scenario:

Mother: "Honey, we'll be leaving to go out of town soon. You need to clean out Fluffy's litter box, make sure there's plenty of food, and oh, could you get that throw up out of the corner that Fluffy put there two days ago?"

Kid: "Sure, Mom, I'd be happy to," (punching a couple of commands into her tiny virtual-responsibility computer). "It's all taken care of." Of course the *actual* throw up is still in the corner and the food dish is still *actually* empty, but the kid is off the hook, because *virtually* she is very responsible.

February 1998

Advice for the April Fool

When my grandpa was studying chemistry in college, he snuck a sulfuric compound from the lab. On one of the busiest nights at the library, he dropped the stuff in a corner, stood back, and watched the entire floor evacuate. The best part of this story is that when I got to college, I talked him into giving me some of the stink compound, of which I deposited a portion in the cafeteria near the salad bar. I got so tickled when people started scurrying towards the door that I had to retreat to my dorm, for fear that I'd be found guilty. I secretly divided the remainder of the compound and randomly deposited it in dorm rooms that were *not* close to mine.

When my papa was in college, he, also a chemistry major, discovered a harmless solution that could turn urine red and spiked the iced tea dispenser with the potion. He said the infirmary was extremely busy for a few hours until someone discovered what had happened. If you're looking for April Fools' pranks and your circle of friends or family doesn't include a mischievous chemist willing to supply you with odious compounds, take heart; I come from a long line of tricksters and have, over the years, gathered and implemented some pranks that can bring about a good laugh even without the use of dubious substances. Molière was of the opinion that "a learned fool is more foolish than an ignorant fool." But April Fools' Day is just a few days away, and, perhaps because of my family's trickery, I'm convinced that a fool can never be too prepared.

My earliest memory of becoming an April Fool is due to my mom's pranks. When I was in grade school, if April first fell on a weekday, my mom would undoubtedly wake my siblings and me at 7:00 AM singing, "Let It Snow, Let It Snow, Let It Snow." She'd report that there was a foot of snow on the ground and that school had been called off. "Get up and look out the window!" she'd coax. I'd bound out of bed to find green grass, daffodils, and sunshine greeting me. *"April Fool!"* she'd yell triumphantly. I fortunately learned well from my elders and inherited, either by genetics or example, a scheming mind.

One April Fools' Day when I was pregnant with my first child, I lowered my standards and used the pregnancy to persuade my husband to serve me, something I said that I would never do. "Honey," I whined as I sat on the couch, "would you please get me a big glass of water? I'm really thirsty and my feet are killing me." Pat immediately went to the sink. "Oh," I sighed, "I just remembered that our water pressure has been terrible today so you have to push the spigot up really fast to get anything out." My unsuspecting husband hadn't realized that I had wrapped a rubber band around the lever of the sink's sprayer hose. When he turned the spigot on full force, his stomach got a cold shower—and my belly, baby and all, got a good laugh!

In college I had the good fortune of being assigned a roomie who was a tad prissier and much more squeamish than I. On April Fools' eve after my roomie had brushed her teeth, I stuffed a dozen raisins into her tube of gel toothpaste. It doesn't take a chemist to know what happens to raisins when they become moist. The raisins did their thing while we slept, and in the morning my roomie got out of bed and headed straight for her toothpaste. "How weird," she said as she attempted to squeeze the tube, "it feels like there's something stuck in here." She pressed a little harder and *plop*, a ball of what could have easily been mistaken for the fecal matter of a deer landed on her toothbrush. She threw the toothpaste at the trash can and ran down the hall screaming that some varmint had defiled her toiletries.

So now you know a few ways to serve up some April first foolishness. Still, you'd be wise to heed one tidbit of advice on how to avoid becoming the brunt of an April Fools' joke: If you see me or any of my family approaching, turn and run the other way. If you don't know what we look like, be alert because you might just become an April Fool.

March 1998

~

Laboring over Labels

Perhaps I don't get out of the house enough. Seems as though there are much more worthy causes to attract my attention than labels, but labels have been items of interest to me lately. There is much competition for my dollar, so marketing companies employ some pretty slick techniques to convince me that throwing my dollar at their company's product will benefit me more than throwing it away on the competitor's product.

I went in search of a perfect pepper grinder. I love cracked pepper on just about everything except toothpaste, but the *gourmet* grinders I had found produced pepper that was too fine. In the grocery store one day I spied a *new* pepper grinder distributed by a spice company, and hey, it worked! The pepper came out in big chunks. I brought it home and set it on the table. After happily spicing my food for a few days, my brother showed up for lunch. He ground a hearty portion of the peppercorns into his soup, spent a few seconds scrutinizing the label, and plopped the pepper back on the table with a "Good grief. It's just pepper."

"Let me see that," I said. Sure enough, to read the label, which contained words such as "attractive," "convenient," "superior quality," "tropical," and "provocative," you'd think the grinder might be more suited to the bedroom than the kitchen table.

I picked up some soft tub butter last month, not the kind I usually get because the store was out of *my* brand. Don't ask why I've succumbed to claiming my own brand. Perhaps my brand offered words of comfort that my cynicism ignored. Once again, I had used the new butter for several days before I discovered the creative writing exercise on the back. The new package, it tells me, gives me 40 percent more servings than any other one pound blend. As far as I can tell, one pound is one pound, no matter how you package it. How can one pound of their butter give me more servings than one pound of my brand unless they've whipped a bunch of air into it? Basically, I'm getting more packaging, more air, and the same amount of butter. I've got to hand it to the writers of those labels. They can make it seem as if the company is a benevolent giver whose product provides all manner of little extras.

How about this one on a favorite cereal of my three year old: a big yellow swatch on the front of the box yells that it's baked with a "touch of brown sugar." Not only that, but the back of the box also hollers about how wholesome and nutritious this cereal is. At least whole wheat is the number one ingredient, but right afterwards is sugar and then brown sugar. What with all the other sugar, I guess there really is just a touch of brown sugar. My grandpa has claimed for years that dog food is more nutritious than breakfast cereal and most other foods marketed to our kids.

It's not just food containers that have been my source of entertainment the last few weeks. On the box of my contact lens solution is an order to read all of the provided information. I know that one really can't be too careful when it comes to eye care. But the provided information, which is the length of a short story, includes a description, actions, indications, contraindications, warnings, precautions, and directions that are all fine printed on the gray inside of the box. I had to remove my contacts after reading the material because of the strain on my eyes. The label instructs me to keep all this info for future use. What exactly would I use it for? Are some people so obedient and organized that they actually read *all* of that information; and once they do, do you suppose they place it in their hygiene products precautions file?

If advertisers were more overtly honest, then at least we could be assured of getting what we're looking for. Why can't my margarine package admit that the taste isn't quite what butter's is but that my arteries will thank me? Should my contact lens box tell me that if I don't read the essay on the inside of the box, I should at least wash my hands before use and store the lenses in fresh solution? Better yet, let's just declare on all food and hygiene product labels, as on all contraceptives, that if you want to keep your waistline and avoid infection, abstinence is your best bet.

March 1997

Lick It, Stick It, and Predict It

It seems that even with such scientific advancements as weather satellites, Doppler radar, and computer imaging, meteorologists have a difficult time predicting the weather. A storm may unexpectedly shift or the wind may suddenly change direction or clouds may slow down and stay put over a particular area or gain momentum and blow away sooner than anticipated.

On January twenty-seventh, light flurries were predicted in the morning, then warming and turning to rain in the afternoon. Asheville, however, got dumped with eight to twelve inches of snow and scattered power outages. Granted, playing in the snow is good for your soul; and heating soup and roasting marshmallows over the fire and reading books to children by candlelight is a worthy lesson in simplicity every now and then. But my focus here is the ability, or lack thereof, to predict.

Case in point: A week later we were told that a few inches of snow were headed our way and that we should brace for another winter storm. The grocery store shelves were wiped clean of milk, but the most the gods could do to accommodate the meteorologists was to spit out a few flurries and then send down rain for a couple of days.

High-tech weather prediction is hopefully more than pure chance, but it reminds me of a doctor my father knew who was famous for being able to prophesy the gender of a fetus. This was before the days of ultrasound technology. This doctor confided to my father that when parents-to-be pressed him relentlessly to disclose the sex of their baby, he would make a prediction. This prediction was purely based on whatever popped into his mind at the moment. Fifty percent of the time this doctor was right and his patients dubbed him a genius. The other 50 percent of the time that he was wrong, people tended to forget about it.

Though we can now determine a baby's gender by three months' gestation, and can sometimes manipulate sperm into creating a boy or a girl, we still cannot control or manipulate the weather and even have difficulty predicting it. Some of the old-fashioned ways of weather forecasting seem nearly as reliable as what our modern equipment presents us with. Licking your finger, sticking it in the air, and noticing which side dries first is an accurate way to determine which way the wind is blowing. Many farmers still plant crops by the *Farmers' Almanac* and will tell you that observing animal behavior and changes in their coats will indicate a change in weather or the length of a season.

My sister, when living in Haiti, learned a valuable lesson about respecting Mother Nature's signs. Jennie and her roommate decided that they would plant banana trees in their yard. They walked into the village and started digging up baby banana trees which shoot up from the mother plant. While they were doing this, a Haitian agricultural trainer whom they knew came by and laughingly said, "You can't do that."

Jennie and Karen, somewhat offended by his snickering and not at all understanding what he meant asked, "You mean we're not *allowed* to dig these up?"

"No, no, no," he answered. "I mean they won't grow if you plant them now—it's the wrong moon."

Jennie and Karen simply responded with a "Yeah, right, whatever." During the forty-five-minute walk through the village back to their house they noticed that everyone along the way stared and laughed at them. Jennie told me that the people weren't being impolite so much as they were just so amazed that someone would actually plant a banana tree in the wrong moon—like planting a geranium here in December. But stubbornly, they persisted. As they were putting the trees in the ground, a neighbor came by and insisted that they shouldn't be planting the trees. Despite the Haitians' best efforts, the trees made it into the ground. Several weeks later the trees died. My sister now asserts that the moon's magnetic pull on the earth is indeed very real and that we in our first-world habitats too often ignore Mother Nature's signs.

So why take the word of a weather professional on television, who is not only inside a room with no windows, but who is also gathering information from a computer and projecting that to you via miles of underground cable? Walk outside, take note of the phase of the moon, lick your finger, and stick it in the air.

March 1998

Curling Iron with an Attitude

Groping recently for a piece of paper to write down a thought, I came across the warranty and product registration card of a curling iron that I purchased last summer. I am sure that in certain cases warranties for household appliances serve a purpose and are actually of benefit to the consumer. But any advantage that a consumer realizes from a contract with a company—which is what a warranty is—has a price. The company, after all, didn't give you their product for free, and most companies won't likely replace an appliance for free when it blows up.

My warranty tells me that if my curling iron is found defective within the warranty period, I must mail it postpaid and properly packaged against possible damage—it seems the company wants me to take good care of their kaput curling iron—to a specified address. Then, the warranty exclaims, "IMPORTANT: Your returned appliance must be accompanied by (a) Proof of Purchase: your bill of sale indicating the purchase date, (b) the completed Service Request Tag indicating the nature of the problem, (c) a check or money order in the amount of four dollars to cover postage, handling, and insurance." But that's not all. My one-year warranty continues, "A return not under warranty is subject to a return fee of twenty-one dollars to cover postage, handling, insurance, and product cost." Isn't that something like blaming the victim? I can understand the company not wanting to replace a curling iron that couldn't withstand the rigors of scraping ice off the windshield of my car or frying grilled cheese sandwiches, but that's not what I use my curling iron for, at least not most of the time.

Warranties may come and go, expiring after a finite period of time, but if you register your product you can be assured of immortality, at least in the world of telemarketing and product promotion. Naturally, the paraphernalia that accompanies my curling iron instructs me to complete the product registration card which declares itself "IMPORTANT!" with big bold lettering. I'm asked to reveal my name, phone number, address, and when and where I purchased my curling iron. My curling iron company also wants to know if I'm married or single, my level of education, my date of birth, the ages of others who live in my house, what my family income is, and finally, if in the last six months I have ever worked in my garden, traveled on vacation, purchased clothes or gifts through the mail, purchased a PC or PC software, purchased two or more books, purchased cassettes or CDs, donated to wildlife or environmental causes, or donated to charities in general. For a moment, I thought I had gotten my product registration card confused with the inquiries of a matchmaking service whose solicitations I receive from time to time. Perhaps the warranty comes with a mail-order date. Finally, in very tiny print at the bottom of the card is a minuscule space between two brackets that I can check if I prefer not to participate in additional market research for my curling iron company or if I choose to deprive myself of information on "new and interesting opportunities" from other companies.

I haven't figured out if actually obtaining a warranty and all its wonderful benefits is contingent on registering a product. You can be sure if you *do* spend your valuable time studying and filling out and sending in the half dozen pieces of paper accompanying your product, that your blender will break down and spew milkshake all over the kitchen two days after the warranty's expiration. Doesn't the useful life of most household appliances expire just after the warranty does? In that manner we at least support capitalism by buying yet another thingamabob—doing our part to keep appliance companies and land fills in business.

In Utopia, appliances would really and truly be built to last a lifetime. But if something *did* go wrong, the consumer could return the broken appliance at the company's expense, and the company, without question, would send a new appliance to a pleased customer. Such a transaction would not be contingent on marital status, income, or whether or not one worked in one's garden during the last six months.

I don't have to tell you this isn't Utopia, but I do like turning the cards in my favor every now and then. If my curling iron is going to ask so much of me, I figure that it can handle the blame when something goes wrong. I burnt myself with my curling iron the other day, and my two year old asked how I'd gotten the big owie on my forehead. I was pleased to lay no claim whatsoever to user error. "Oh," I told him nonchalantly, "my curling iron has an attitude."

April 1998

~

Great-grandpa's Advertisement

My great-grandfather, Clyde E. Smith, began a drugstore in my hometown of Rutledge, Tennessee, at the turn of the century. While I was home on a recent visit, my father went rummaging through his old roll-top desk and pulled from underneath stacks of forgotten papers and worn pencils a folded, yellowed clipping from the *Grainger County News* announcing the drugstore's twenty-fifth anniversary in 1930.

The discovery of this tattered announcement uncovered some literary genius in one of my predecessors of which I wasn't previously aware. My great-grandfather reveals a remarkable play with language. He also expresses a genuine fondness for the people whom he served in what could easily have been an ordinary business anniversary announcement of "We're twenty-five years old; come in and help us celebrate." Clyde's humorous advertisement reads as follows:

Twenty-Fifth Anniversary

For a quarter of a century I have been hunting for thrills, selling pills, looking at empty tills, and paying bills to relieve the ills of my fellow man. My eats have been short of meats, met all kinds of cheats, repeats, and dead beats. Have been debated, agitated, aggravated, and placated. Have sinned, been skinned, and grinned. Have cussed and discussed. Talked to and talked about, lied to and lied about, held up and held down, squeezed, and bulldozed. Have been bawled out and balled up, besotted and boycotted. Have been baptized, criticized, and ostracized, stuck for war tax, dog tax, and syntax. Have given to the Red Cross, green cross, and double cross. Subscribed for Liberty bonds, baby bonds, and still retain my matrimonial bonds. Have contributed to worthy and unworthy causes. Joined several reliefs even to stomach relief. Been robbed until about busted and disgusted. Have worked like the devil and been worked worse than that. Yet, it has been a pleasure to serve you. I appreciate your confidence and friendship and I ask that when in need of anything that a good drugstore sells to call on me and I promise that I will beg, borrow, or steal anything that will make for your health, happiness, and prosperity.

Remember that I will be sticking around, come in and laugh with me or at me but for God's sake *laugh.*

Your Druggist
Clyde E. Smith
Rutledge, Tennessee

This yellowed clipping from the *Grainger County News* caused me to miss a man whom I never knew. I found myself wishing that my great-grandpa were still "sticking around" in his store so that we could sit down at the old marble-and-glass-top fountain, order Coke floats, and share laughs. But in a very real sense, he is still here—after all I did have a good chuckle when I read the store's anniversary announcement. Clyde's adage gave me something I didn't expect—the gift of knowing that I can pass on, through my writing, a little humor, lightness of spirit, and balance to those who might one day find themselves glancing over words I have penned. Not only did Great-grandpa brighten my day, but also, by his example, he demonstrated a way for me to achieve a little immortality.

Wherever Clyde is, I hope he realizes that those who knew him and those of us who were never fortunate enough to know him, appreciate the lengths to which he would go to satisfy his customers, in particular dispensing humor along with prescriptions. Today I, along with my parents and siblings, aunts, uncles, cousins, and our children, do laugh often and loud together. Maybe, just maybe, Great-grandpa hears us.

June 1998

The Computer Wouldn't Let Me Do It

A couple of weeks ago I phoned in an order for pizza and requested a large one-topping with half mushrooms and half extra cheese. "That counts as a two-topping pizza," the perky pizza person who answered the phone informed me.

"But it's half of each topping," I countered.

"Oh, I know it doesn't make sense," she offered apologetically, "but the computer won't let me do half and half as a one-topping." I wondered if perky pizza person had given up her own cognitive skills to that of a computer.

"Think for yourself!" I wanted to yell. "How difficult can it be to tell the pizza makers that I want a half-and-half and then charge me for only a one topping?" But because she was so friendly and seemed convinced of the computer's omnipotence, I gave in and changed my order a little to accommodate the computer and to not confuse the perky pizza person. Still, I remained insulted by the computer's ability to sway the flavor of my dinner that evening. I kept wondering whether, in this age of superinformation, people control computers or whether computers control people. I promised myself that I would soon write a commentary on "My Top Ten Pet Peeve Excuses," of which the phrase "the computer won't let me do it" would be number one.

Then, my computer took over my life. It started when my husband and I decided we would upgrade our embarrassingly antiquated four-year-old system to a state-of-the-art multi-media station with a CD-ROM player, a sound card, and speakers—and, frugal as we are, we would do it all by ourselves. Six days later both Pat and I were in sleep debt, as our evening social life had consisted of staring bleary-eyed into a monitor, banging out commands on a keyboard, rearranging cables in the guts of the computer, and spending hours on the telephone with technical assistants.

When we finally got the sound-card software installed, we managed to screw it up the next night while attempting to correct a problem we thought the CD-ROM software had created. On the following night when attempting to correct the problem with the sound-card software, we lost our entire Windows environment. Following that mishap, I forgot my scruples and spoke to a technical support person as though he were a marriage counselor for couples who are breaking up because a computer has come between them. "How many divorces have you known computers to cause?" I queried expectantly.

He only laughed and offered a reassuring, "Oh, that won't happen to *you*."

However, with the absence of the Windows environment, I was thrown into a panic. Though not entirely his fault, I fussed at my husband with questions of, "How am I gonna get my commentary written? How am I gonna do the research I needed to do on-line? *How will I function?*" Around midnight that evening I found myself jealously eyeing the cat who was entirely oblivious to any benefit or harm the computer might dole out. "What's it like to live without having to put up with a computer?" I asked her out loud.

I promise you that the cat offered a look of "Well, *I* can nap anytime I feel like it," and trotted off to her favorite snoozing spot.

At least the computer's attempt at making my life miserable for a solid week resulted in my remembering the old-fashioned way to write—with a pencil and a piece of paper. I dug through our stack of dusty computer-reference books for a notepad, and I found myself actually able to write by forming the letters with a pencil. That's how this commentary got started. I know it's an outdated concept, and it was much slower than clicking away at a keyboard. I really wanted to go online and conduct some research on a meaningful public-interest topic, organize my ideas into neat little files in Word, and compose a gripping, well-thought-out comment the fast, modern way at my enhanced multimedia station. But the dad-gum computer just wouldn't let me do it.

June 1997

~

The Maternity Suit and Boot Company

I stared at the flimsy, trendy hiking boots decorating the wall of the shoe store. "Do you have any decent boots for women that don't have aqua and pink splashed all over them?" I asked the clean-cut high-school-aged sales boy who was helping me. He looked stunned—as if I were the only woman on the face of the universe to ever request hiking boots that look like they're made for the trails instead of something that came straight out of Barbie's closet. I half-expected him to attempt a hard sell and enthusiastically exclaim that the women's boots did come with free matching nail and lip color.

He only offered an apologetic, "Uh, no ma'am, I don't believe we do."

"Well, I want some serious hiking boots, and I'm not planning on wearing them with lace socks," I reminded him. The sales boy smiled—at least he thought my quest for a real pair of hiking boots was amusing—and I smiled back. After all, he wasn't the one who had designed these boots to look as if they were meant to be color coordinated with a specific outfit and make-up line.

I'll admit that I'm full of contradictions—especially when it comes to clothing. While I don't want flimsy pink hiking boots, I do want a breezy swimsuit in bright colors. I especially wanted lightweight material and splashy colors when I was pregnant. Anyone who has spent time around a pregnant woman in the summer (or fall or winter or spring, for that matter) knows that the body temperature of pregnant women is about twenty degrees above everybody else's, and that their feet and ankles tend to swell and ache. In this regard, pregnant women will expend a lot of energy trying to keep cool and comfortable. When I was pregnant I wanted little more than to prop up my feet in a sixty-degree room and sit motionless in front of a fan.

So when I went searching for a swimsuit for my ever-expanding belly, I was surprised. Maternity swimwear came in a full range of drab: brown, gray, navy, and black. Perhaps to make my fattening tummy look thinner? I wanted fuchsia and yellow and chartreuse and flowers—lots of flowers, to celebrate my baby while I lay sunning my big-bellied self at the beach.

Maternity swimsuits, as I discovered, were not designed with the concepts of cool or comfort or fashion in mind. I found swimwear with a neckline that actually covered the neck. I tried on bathing suits that were careful to completely cover my expectant thighs and bowing back. Yards and yards of sweaty-looking material went into fashioning panels and layers of fabric to fit over my tummy—as if the sight of a pregnant woman at the beach or pool comes dangerously close to revealing where babies really come from. The price of this confining piece of cloth was about seventy bucks—all that money for a swimsuit I *might* wear one season. I finally revealed to the mature sales woman assisting me that I needed something a lot brighter and a little cheaper. "Oh, but our prices are as good as any specialty shop," she said, trying to sound reassuring, "and we carry almost the full range of colors for *maternity* swimsuits."

I must say that at that moment, I had an absolutely brilliant idea. If the manufacturers of women's hiking boots and the makers of maternity swimwear collaborated, pregnant people would have some fun, comfortable, wearable clothes. All that the companies would have to do is simply swap material and design ideas. In this way the former maternity swimsuit company could construct sturdy, brown hiking boots that would cover the entire foot and ankle and last almost a lifetime. The former women's boot company could adequately throw together breezy swimsuits in bright, trendy colors that would comfortably grace the bellies of expectant moms. It wouldn't hurt business to swap sales personnel either. The mature, common-sense saleswoman would be great outfitting women in hiking boots, and the fun-loving, albeit shy, high-school boy would be fabulous selling floral maternity swimsuits.

In my expecting days, I certainly would've given the Maternity Suit and Boot Company my business. I would have felt fantastic plodding off to the pool in my dark brown hiking boots and prissy, daisy-covered belly.

July 1998

Margarita Ice and Coffee Biscotti Chocolatti

My husband and I want to expand our children's horizons and broaden their tastes. So we've tried to teach our kids to enjoy different kinds of foods, and for the most part, our efforts have worked. When we go to a Mexican restaurant, our children gobble up enchiladas. When we eat Chinese, they dig into tofu and steamed dumplings. At Japanese restaurants, our five year old orders sushi, and our three year old goes for shrimp.

I never expected their eclectic tastes to spill over into the world of ice cream. On a recent visit to an ice cream shop my kids ignored the Kids Only section that contained brightly colored flavors with names such as Zoolicious Ocean Swirl and Bubble Gum. Maybe it was sensory overload, but I was attempting to be conventional for once and tried to coax my three year old into strawberry ice cream. I don't know why I expected such of him. I myself never pick the conventional strawberry, chocolate, or vanilla when I'm in an ice cream shop. I choose something rich and decadent like French vanilla cream with chocolate caramel swirls or an exotic mango watermelon twist—you know, something you can't get every day on the grocer's shelves.

My three year old of course paid about as much attention to me as he had to the kids' section. "I want to try that green kind," he said, pointing toward the adult low-fat section, at a tub of Margarita Ice.

"*That* green kind?" I asked. "Not this mint green over here or the vanilla with green marshmallow squiggles in it?"

"No, Mommy," he said patiently, and a little too clearly, "that kind, the Margarita Ice."

I winked knowingly at the high-school girl behind the counter. "Let us have a *little* taste of Margarita Ice," I indulged, figuring that once the tart margarita flavor landed on Blaise's tongue he'd immediately go for the sweet Rainbow Blast in the kids' section. She smiled and handed Blaise a teensy spoon buried under a half scoop of greenish Margarita Ice. Blaise tasted, grinned, and tasted some more.

"Oh, I like it, Mommy," he exclaimed. The ice-cream girl grinned bigger.

"Okay," I consented, "we'll take a *child-size* scoop of Margarita Ice."

I joined up with my husband and our five year old. "Look what Blaise picked out," I told him.

"Look what Gabe got," my husband retorted. Our five year old was inhaling a bowl of Coffee Biscotti Chocolatti.

This was encouraging, as our parental epicurean wisdom obviously was being heeded. Somehow, though, my Coconut ice cream and my husband's Peanut Butter Chocolate Chip tasted ever-so-slightly bland.

July 1999

Cool Godzilla

Memorial Day weekend I was innocently minding my own business in the grocery store, concentrating on recalling my list, which I had left at home. Was it milk, cheese, and bread I darted in the store for or milk, bananas, and tea? At least I had remembered the milk, and in heading for the milk aisle, I passed the ice cream. While trying to recall if I needed to pick up some ice cream too, I eyed big lizards plastered to half-gallon ice-cream cartons. "That's curious," I thought, "lizard ice cream." A closer look revealed that it wasn't just plain ol' boring lizard ice cream, but *Godzilla* ice cream. Then I gathered from the hype surrounding the frozen dessert section of the grocery store that *Godzilla: The Movie* would soon be hitting theaters *everywhere*. Honestly, this was the first I had heard of the movie. Then everywhere I turned it seemed Godzilla stuff had infected stores like a vicious virus. There was Godzilla cereal, Godzilla pasta, Godzilla toys, Godzilla T-shirts, Godzilla lunch boxes, and God-zilla only knows what else.

All the frenzy irritated me. I felt left behind on the beach while the rest of the world went sailing past on the Godzilla luxury liner. You see, until I started discovering lizards in food and clothes and toys, I thought Godzilla was a gorilla. In a curious way, I had melded the destructive forces of a mutant lizard with the rage of a misunderstood overgrown ape, thus confusing Godzilla and King Kong. Obviously, I don't watch much TV, I don't subscribe to the newspaper, and I don't listen to the radio. Except of course for WNCW—partly because this station doesn't play Godzilla movie commercials or yell at me between songs about how I need to buy my kid a remote-control spear-throwing plastic Godzilla that requires four "D" batteries.

Still, even if I were a fan of terrible giant lizards, my rebel side would surely have resisted the hype and hoopla of Godzilla-mania. Throughout the Godzilla days of summer, I made sure that our meals contained no Godzilla products. When my family ate spaghetti, it was long and stringy like worms, not streamlined and scaly like lizards. Our ice cream had a picture of ice cream on the carton, not a picture of a giant lizard eating Manhattan. Our breakfast cereal even maintained a simple O shape, not sharp-toothed lizard profiles with skyscraper marshmallows.

As for clothes, my kids wore sharks and dinosaurs and bugs and alligators this summer but not Godzilla. Heck, we don't even own Godzilla underwear or bedroom shoes shaped like lizard feet. My kids watch PBS so they didn't see Godzilla commercials on TV, and Godzilla was conspicuous only by its absence in my kids' books and toys. My husband and I had sufficiently enclosed our boys in an anti-Godzilla bubble. My children, bless their hearts, were deprived to our satisfaction.

Godzilla: The Movie has now come and gone—going as fast as it came. Still, the paraphernalia lingers. Just last week in the grocery store my two year old darted for the toys, immediately picked up a Godzilla doll (on sale of course), and exclaimed, "Look, Mommy, a dinosaur!" I proudly congratulated myself on successfully administering a shot in the arm to all the penetrating consumerism, media-ism, and commercialism that had attempted to convince my kids that Godzilla is the coolest thing since Beanie Babies and virtual pets.

"My kids don't recognize Godzilla at all," I thought. "They think Godzilla is merely a prehistoric giant lizard." I couldn't wait to tell my husband that our efforts at keeping Godzilla from gobbling up our children were not in vain.

Then my ever-wise four year old chimed in, "That's not a dinosaur," he explained importantly and with a sense of secrecy, "that's *Godzilla!*" With one penetrating look he revealed to his little brother that he would soon, in their secret hiding place, far away from their busy-bodying parents, disclose to his eager understudy all the forbidden nuances and idiosyncrasies that kids everywhere know, respect, and revere about Godzilla—the giant lizard that squeezes through your front door and then grows too immense to push out.

August 1998

~

It's Football Time from Here to Detroit

We were mundanely drying the breakfast dishes on a late-summer Saturday when Pat let me in on a little secret. "Well," he said with a sparkle in his eyes and a big grin plastered to his face, "just think, in one more week . . ." This is the sort of thing my husband says when he's really looking forward to something. "Just think," he'll say, "in one week we'll be hitting the rapids on the New River!" or,

"Just think, in one week we'll be eating seafood at the beach."

That morning's "just think" announcement somehow held a little more enthusiasm than in the past. In the silent few seconds that followed, my mind swarmed with thoughts of lying under a palm on a Jamaican beach or of taking in the Mediterranean atmosphere of Malta. "Wow," I thought, "he's planned an early anniversary celebration for us and has already bought plane tickets and made arrangements for the kids!"

I looked expectantly at my husband, then I heard, "One week from today, it's the beginning of . . . *football season*!"

"Have fun," I pouted. "I'll be in Detroit."

I later shared with a friend the way Pat broke it to me—the way he just could not squelch his delight and the way that I just could not bust out jumping for joy. I thought my friend would sympathize with my frustration at Pat's obvious lack of interest in the Caribbean or Mediterranean at this time of year. I couldn't help revealing to my friend what I thought was my witty comeback about Detroit. My friend looked sheepishly at me and replied, "You know, that might not be such a bad idea. Detroit's supposed to have a good team this year."

I tried to get interested. Honest. Last year I went to a U.T. game with my sister, brother, dad, and husband. We had a pregame picnic near Neyland Stadium, and between bites of food we'd yell "Go Vols!" as people with orange clothes, orange faces, and orange hair drove past us in their orange cars. We then squeezed past the overly zealous college students to find our seats in the stadium. The band high-stepped in and performed a rousing, as if the crowd needed rousing, pregame show. The cheerleaders and players dashed onto the field. The orange crowd exploded and did the wave and I was hyped. "Yes," I thought, "this *is* fun."

Then the game began. After the kickoff my attention quickly faded into the roar of the crowd. I struck up a conversation with a ten-year-old girl sitting behind me who was enamored with my fingernails that I had painted alternately orange and white. I leaned my head on the railing and attempted a catnap. I bought a Coke for its caffeine value. That proving futile, I leafed through a program that someone in my party had invested in and tried to find an article of interest, but to no avail. The game dragged on until, finally, it was over.

I don't remember who we played or even whether we won or lost. The important thing is that after the game ended, life once again held excitement for me. We poured out of the stadium in a sea of orange—as we had come in. We flowed along to my dad's car and piled in. Papa cranked up the original "Rocky Top," and a couple of us hung out of the sunroof dancing to a banjo beat as we headed out of downtown Knoxville.

Still, this season I think I'll just go to Detroit.

September 1998

~

One Pickup Truck, Not for Sale

It's not often that something causes me to slow down when I'm driving. I like to go fast. In my previous life I must have been a race-car driver. But as I jetted past a small house on a back road one day, something grabbed me, making me take pause and think.

In the yard of this little house sat a red and white pickup truck. Now even though I was driving race cars around in my other life, and although I sometimes drive a small blue Nissan truck, I'm no expert when it comes to pickups. Sure, I could probably pick one out of the crowd that's extraordinary either by virtue of being an antique or being new and fancy with lots of bells and whistles. This particular red and white truck in the yard of this little house fell into neither of these categories. It was a Chevrolet, maybe a mid-eighties model, nothing all that spectacular. But the thing that caught my eye was the wording on the windshield. In huge, white shoe-polish letters it announced, "NOT FOR SALE!" complete with an exclamation mark. As if everybody who drove by stopped in to inquire whether they might buy this remarkable vehicle! I'm used to seeing shoe-polish letters that tell me why I *should* buy a particular car or truck, but to tell me that I shouldn't even be asking about this one was another matter all together.

I asked my husband if he had seen the truck that wasn't for sale on his way to work. "I probably see lots of trucks that aren't for sale on my way to work," he said suspiciously, as if I might be trying to sneakily convince him that we need a new truck.

"Yeah," I said, "but I'm talking about the one that tells you outright that you can't buy it." He claimed not to have seen it, still eyeing me questionably.

I wanted to stop in at that little house to ask the people there why I couldn't buy their truck, but the "NOT FOR SALE!" sign wasn't exactly an invitation to go knocking on their door, so I shied away. They had a car in the yard beside the truck, again nothing exciting. The car, though, didn't have shoe-polish letters on it. I wondered if it might be available. Not that I wanted it; I was just curious, but I didn't ask.

Still, I was hoping to figure out why these people were advertising that their truck wasn't for sale. Maybe reverse psychology, I thought. To say that it's unavailable might make it much more appealing, in a twisted kind of way. But there was no phone number to call if indeed you didn't want to buy the truck, and certainly no red carpet of welcome to inquire inside about how much, hypothetically speaking, the truck wouldn't be if you couldn't buy it.

My brother has been sort of in the market for another vehicle for about a year now. I wanted to show him the truck that he couldn't have one day. We drove past the little house, but the truck was gone. No sign of it at all.

"Maybe they didn't sell it already," he said, a little disappointed. I reassured him. He was, after all, the one who didn't buy it, and that's what the previous owners were looking for, or not.

October 1999

I Like Cheese

My mom, by nature of having birthed four kids, is quick to give out advice. This trait, that can be annoying to those of us with the title of daughter or son, does on occasion prove to be beneficial, as my mom has recently struck gold in the mine of advice giving. Though I haven't had the opportunity to use the helpful information she has doled out, my husband, if you can believe it, was actually very quick to heed his mother-in-law's advice.

To honestly be in need of advice, one must have a problem. My problem is how to get rid of telemarketers. When I get a call on a Friday night to tell me how much I need accidental death insurance from Sears, I'm not amused and am even less willing to fork over my money. What do they expect people to say? "Oh yes, I'm so glad you called. As I was sitting here with my beer and unwinding from a hectic week, it suddenly occurred to me that I need more accidental death insurance than I already have, and since I'm too lazy to contact my own insurance agent about it, I was hoping someone like you, who is obviously concerned about my family's well-being should I pass on, would take it upon himself to give me a call."

Like me, perhaps many of you are wondering how to rid yourselves of these pesky calls without resorting to breaking the phone or sharing with the caller all the four-letter expletives you learned in junior high, which your kids will inevitably hear and repeat at the most embarrassing moments possible. I've even thought about changing my listing to the cat's name so that whenever anyone calls and tries to sell vinyl siding to Fluffy I'll know it's safe to hang up.

My mom, knowing that I've been in need of the getting-rid-of-telemarketers advice for quite some time, one day asked triumphantly, "Do you want to know how to get a telemarketer to hang up on you?" I was a little hesitant. My mom was actually asking me if I wanted her advice, instead of giving it out freely, and I found myself admitting that I needed it. "All you have to do," she offered quickly before I could change my mind, "is say 'I like cheese.'"

"I like cheese?" I questioned.

"Yeah, and it works!" she bragged. She told me that she had received a call from a man wanting her to buy some stock. After he finished his first few sentences, she asked, "Do you like cheese?" He came up with a stunned, "Uh, yeah," then continued his spiel at which point she stated, "I like cheese." My mom said that he paused for a moment and kept on. Then, as my mom put it, "I interrupted and told him again that I like cheese, and *he* hung up on *me!* It was wonderful!"

It *does* work. My husband tried it with a woman who called to politely inform us that her computer showed that we don't subscribe to our local newspaper. "No, but I like cheese," my husband offered. There was a pause while she looked at her script for a response to that one, then she formulated an "Oh, that's strange" on her own, then, "Would you like to subscribe?"

"No, but I like cheese." Another pause, then the triumphant click.

The only real danger in this cheese thing is if your four year old overhears the conversation, as ours did, which on his end sounds something like this: Phone ringing. His supposedly mature father answering with a "Hello." Then, "I like cheese . . . I like cheese . . . I like cheese." Followed by hanging up the phone and a round of laughter by both parents. Naturally Gabe reasoned that this cheese thing must be pretty cool. The next time he got on the phone with my mom, his end of the conversation, very closely approximated my husband's approach with the telemarketer:

Granny: "Hi, Gabe. How are you?"

Gabe: "I like cheese."

Granny [Laughing, proud that her grandson is being trained to follow in her footsteps]: "I know you like cheese. I do too. So how was preschool today?"

Gabe [With a silly laugh]: "I like cheese."

There is one other tiny problem, but I'm sure my mom will discover a creative way to prevent those telemarketers from selling your phone number to cheese companies. When she does, I'll pass the advice on to you.

November 1997

The Game

I'm no avid fan, but I occasionally enjoy a good football game. Crisp fall air seems to soften my skepticism of the sport. The recent Tennessee/Alabama game had me watching, which will probably be the only game that I view in its entirety this season. I watched partly because I'm from Tennessee; partly because I did actually want to see the Vols beat Bama; and partly because my husband had taped the game, and we could fast forward through the commercials. Aside from all that, the game itself merited being watched, with Tennessee making a great comeback in the second half. I shall acknowledge, however, that I am, for the most part, oblivious to football, even in the midst of a family whose blood runs bright orange.

In a conversation with my mother following the game, she claimed to be so frustrated at half time that she went into the kitchen slamming cabinet doors and slinging dishes around. I must say that my mom is spunky, but hey, she's got grandkids. Not to be generationally biased, but how many grannies do you know who abuse their kitchens because of a football game? I do admire her passion.

Speaking of passion, I phoned my sister, who lives in Knoxville, two days after the game. "What the heck happened to your voice?" I asked. She's not a smoker, but she sure sounded as though she had puffed away at an entire carton of Swisher Sweets. "*The game!*" she rasped.

"I didn't think you went," I said.

"I didn't, I watched it on TV."

"You did that to your vocal cords sitting in front of a TV?" I questioned.

"Heck, yeah," she said, "you should have heard me *yesterday*—I couldn't talk at all." My sister then confessed to threatening bodily harm to an innocent friend passing by the TV set who flatly remarked more than once that it was "just a game."

My father, perhaps sensing the threatening weather on the Saturday that the Tide rolled into Knoxville, offered his tickets to my brother and his friend who actually stayed for the whole game, in spite of torrents of rain. Papa viewed the game from the warmth and dryness of his couch, yet threw creative expletives at the screen as though he were the one irritated by soppy clothes.

Even my husband, who is from Nebraska and is a true Husker, was pulling for the Vols in a big way. Pat tends to be much more mild mannered than I. But I found this calm, serene, and normally sane husband of mine squirming on the edge of the couch and cracking his knuckles as though he were watching *Arachnophobia* again. Nor did Pat refrain from tossing colorful tidbits of advice to the refs and players. I found myself talking back to the commentators, critiquing their use of the English language and telling them to please be quiet for just a couple of minutes. "Good grief," I said, "to hear them talk, you'd think the whole University of Tennessee revolved around Peyton Manning's existence."

"Lee Ann," Pat huffed, "quit being such an anti-football fan." So I decided to put aside my cynicism and try participating in the game.

To show some solidarity with my team, I complained that where the refs placed the ball didn't make any sense, but that prompted a lesson from Pat on how downs and penalties work. When Tennessee's quarterback got clobbered a few times, I proudly recognized that he had been rushed and whined, "That's not right, they're not supposed to rush! I thought you weren't allowed to rush!"

"Honey," Pat sighed, "that's only when we play football in the yard with your family."

"Oh. Okay," I admitted.

My family knows that every bit of what I know about football could fit on the tip of a cleat, but they still let me play in their backyard games. I'm given complete instructions on where to run, when to throw, who to guard and tackle, and what it takes to keep the ball. Not much unlike the guys in the shoulder pads and tight pants, don't you think?

I can tell you this: *playing* the game with Tennessee fans is a lot more friendly than *watching* them watch the Vols play.

November 1996

~

The Vote That Almost Was

There's a lot that bugs me about the political system in this county: lobbying, pork barrel spending, worthy bills that are vetoed because they contain leechy private-interest clauses, the amount of money that it takes to conduct a political campaign. Still, when it comes right down to it, I'm proud to be living in a place where voting is a right. I am allowed to have some control, no matter how minute it may be, over who is running the country. While living in China, I observed to what extent people are willing to sacrifice just to express their opinions on a political issue, so I vote when election time rolls around.

This year, I researched the candidates. At least I skimmed the political flyers that cluttered my mailbox before I tossed them in the recycling bin, and I read an e-mail on the qualifications of the state candidates that a friend forwarded to me. Since we don't subscribe to the newspaper, I quizzed my husband on what he had read about the candidates in the paper at work. That was basically my research, but I figure it was better than going into the voting booth and punching a button corresponding to a cool-sounding name. At any rate, I felt as informed as I've ever been for a nonpresidential year election. I actually had some pretty strong feelings about some of the candidates.

On November third, I headed for the polls, my three year old and five year old in tow. A poll worker escorted me to the booth and explained the procedure. I wanted to make sure that I registered my educated decisions properly so I presented my escort with a question.

"What if I select a candidate by accident?" I asked. During her patient explanation of how to make a correction, the entire machine seemed to lose power.

"What was that?" I asked, expecting that I had gotten a dud booth.

The poll lady glanced down at my three year old. "Uh, he must have punched this big square button here. I'm afraid he just voted for you," she offered apologetically.

"But I didn't have anybody selected yet," I argued desperately. "Can't I vote again?"

"I'm sorry," the poll lady said, "you only get one chance." As if I *wanted* to vote three or four times!

"But that was his vote, not mine," I whined. She offered me a blank look. So I asked if there was any way to tell who I'd just voted for.

"No, we can't retrieve that information," the poll lady explained, sounding as if my two kids and I might be stretching her patience a bit. So Blaise got a speech and we went home.

That night when my husband and I were watching the election returns, I found myself feeling as though I had actually contributed something to the decisions being made. "Oh, look," I said contentedly, "that guy I was gonna vote for is winning!"

"Well, I *did* vote for that guy and he's winning," Pat pointed out.

"Oh yeah, well, I tried," I fussed defensively.

I told my mom about the incident and also got no sympathy from her. Being the granny that she is, she was quite impressed. "Well, Blaise doesn't have to wait until *he* is eighteen to vote," she exclaimed proudly.

I thought about calling my representative to demand that child care be implemented at each polling station, but by the time such a measure makes it to the voters, Blaise will likely be eighteen, and his vote would probably just cancel mine out anyway.

November 1998

Standard Time Jet Lag

I've got jet lag. My appetite is waning. My eyes are puffy. I'm a little dizzy. Unfortunately I haven't been on a long and exotic trip. I haven't even been on a long trip. I can't brag about how my system is all messed up thanks to crossing the international date line when returning from Tahiti. I can't concede that a little bit of jet lag is a small price to pay for having nothing to do but sip piña coladas on the beach, snorkel during the day, and feast on lobster at night. I went to my brother's Halloween party on Saturday night. It was a trip, but I can't really count that because it took me only fifteen minutes to drive to his place.

My jet lag is due to having to switch to standard time. When I returned home from the party, my husband reminded me that we'd get an extra hour's sleep that night. We stayed up late reading. Ah, what a luxury, I thought, almost as good as Tahiti. We put our books down, turned out the light and looked at the clock: 12:00. We reminded ourselves that this translated to 11:00 in the new time. I closed my eyes, dreaming of tropical drinks and warm sun. The only problem was that we forgot to remind our children that we were slated to get an extra hour's sleep.

Our kids, for reasons unbeknownst to Dr. Spock, the laws of common sense, and the modern scientific community, are early risers. By early risers I mean that they usually get up between 6:30 and 7:00, on purpose. This is approximate. On Saturdays and Sundays they're usually up by 6:15 making sure that the remote-control Tonka truck can still go careening down the hall and bang into Mommy and Papa's bedroom door. On school days, they have been known to sleep past 7:00. I must then wake my older child, dress him while he's shoveling oatmeal into his mouth, and send him toward the bus with sleep still in his eyes.

This past Sunday morning at precisely 5:15, we heard giggles. My husband and I moaned. The kids were bright-eyed and bushy-tailed. We ended up gaining our hour *after* Mr. Sandman had left the house for the day. I can't really blame my kids. They were just listening to their biological clocks, clocks that don't respect the intellectual attempt to toy with linear time. My kids aren't to blame for my jet lag, either. It's not their fault that all this week I've wanted to sleep at lunch and do lunch at bedtime.

If you've made the journey into standard time successfully, I offer you my sincerest congratulations. My trip through this new time zone has left me longing for the good ol' days of last week when my kids slept until 6:30, and it didn't get late so early. I'm reluctantly abiding by the new time, a little like a scolded child who will sit in time-out. The lesson I'm learning is patience, because my husband and I know that the only way we will recoup our lost hour is to wait patiently for daylight savings time. By then our kids will have adjusted to standard time, so when they wake up at 6:30, it'll really be 7:30. *Then* we will have slept in.

November 1999

~

My Stat

It's that time—time for my annual football commentary. I know you await this piece with much anticipation, since I am, after all, such an expert on the subject. Hey, before you laugh too hard, I can throw you a stat that I learned a few weekends ago: Wyoming's quarterback got sacked thirteen times by Tennessee. There, see, I do know something about football.

Sometime during the ten minutes that I spent watching the game, an announcer mentioned that little tidbit of information, and, for some reason, I didn't forget it. Don't ask me why. I can't remember important numbers that my kids often quiz me on, such as how many feet there are in a mile or how many miles light can travel in one second or how many light-years it would take to get to Jupiter. But I know that my homeboys sacked Wyoming's quarterback thirteen times. I'm proud that I've retained this small portion of football fact. It has allowed me to exact some slight revenge.

To say that I'm on the periphery of football talk is a gross politeness. During football conversations I'm completely ignored. People don't bother to talk over me or around me or through me. If football is mentioned, I'm not in the picture. It's as if everyone in the room has received a post-hypnotic suggestion that makes me invisible to them. That is unless somebody decides the conversation needs a lift and says, "Hey, remember that time that Lee Ann wanted to know who Peyton Manning was?" or, "Heh, heh, heh, what about that time she called a field goal a touchdown!" As I've mentioned before, everything I know about football could fit on the tip of a cleat. Except now I know that Wyoming's quarterback got sacked thirteen times. This little morsel of scrumptious fact waited patiently on my tongue until just the right moment.

A couple of days after the Tennessee/Wyoming game, it made itself known. I was having lunch with my extended family—die-hard Tennessee fans who were discussing the game in earnest detail. I had been invisible for some time, sipping silently on my soup while football words bounced back and forth across the dining room table. It sounded like this: "Bluh bluh bloo blah, Tee Martin; Bluh bluh bloo blah, Coach Fulmer; Bluh bluh bloo blah bunch of woosies."

I latched onto the "bunch of woosies" part because that was in a language I could understand. I sat up straight, cleared my throat, and opened my mouth. "Well, Wyoming's quarterback got sacked thirteen times. I don't think that's too shabby."

My brother looked as if God had just announced that he or she was going to color the world orange. There was a deep silence of several seconds. "Hey, throwin' out some

U.T. stats there, aren't ya, Sis?" my brother declared, obviously extremely impressed. I grinned humbly.

But the humble part was a facade. I was determined to remember that Wyoming's quarterback got sacked thirteen times well into next season, and I'd pull it out when need be to show what an expert I was on the subject of football. Just the other day my husband and brother were discussing the virtues of a Florida State defeat. "Yeah," I chimed in, "anything's possible. After all, Wyoming's quarterback got sacked thirteen times." They gave each other knowing glances, and—poof!—I was out of the picture once again. Gotta find another stat.

September 1999

Life's Not-so-little Lessons

"[My family] never got up from the table to go watch TV or to do other things. We always sat around and talked about the day or what was happening. One meal could almost go into the next by the time we'd sit around and just talk."

—Storyteller
CONNIE REGAN-BLAKE
of Asheville, North Carolina

Let It Snow!

Winter's first snowfall finds me running outside like a six year old with my opened mouth tilted towards the heavens trying to catch snowflakes on my tongue. As the ground becomes whiter, I coax my young sons, who look on in bewilderment, into plopping into the snow, and we lie on our backs making snow angels.

But, other than students who think they might get out of school, the general population doesn't seem to go cartwheeling when forecasters announce that snow is on the way. There are, however, a good deal of us who love snow, so why must weather announcers preface their snowy predictions with "Sorry folks, I've got some bad news . . ." or, "I hate to be the one tell you but . . ."? I realize that driving can be a mess, schools close, you might be stuck in your house for a day or two, and that bread and milk disappear from the grocer's shelves. So hey, grab a beer and make yourself a tortilla sandwich. I'm going to suggest some ways that, if you do get stuck with snow, you can enjoy it. These activities are great, not just for you and your kids, but for you and your buddies or you and the neighborhood kids—anyone who needs a break from suggestions of snowy gloom and doom.

1. **Make snow cream**
   At three or more inches of snow I scurry to isolated patches around our house and taste test little bits. If I detect a smoky taste, the patch fails, and, as everyone knows, yellow patches are avoided. If a plot passes quality control, I run inside for my big yellow Pyrex bowl and a giant spoon, then return to the blue-ribbon patch, pick out pine needles, and fill the

bowl full of snow. Back inside, I whip up a concoction of eggs, sugar, evaporated milk, and vanilla, gradually add the snow, and *voilà*—snow cream! Even those of you that are skeptical about snow can surely learn to love it this way. It makes a yummy bedtime snack.

2. **Make snow cones**
   Provide your kids with the previously mentioned snow-inspection tips, give them plastic cups and an assignment of hard packing snow into the cups. When they finish packing, pour grape juice over the snow, hand your kids a spoon and a straw, and watch them gobble, as you're slurping away at yours, of course.

3. **Make your driveway or yard the neighborhood ski run**
   Keep the sand in your sandbox, forget about your shovel. If your spouse is resistant to the idea, argue for the health and well-being that will be promoted when those in the vicinity hear squeals of laughter coming from your yard. If you don't live on a hill, seek out a neighbor's sloping lot (with permission of course). Put the pleasure principle of snow to the ultimate test in a sled (those round, plastic saucers are super) or an inflatable float or a trash bag. Heck, I've even sledded on an old car hood before, but I wouldn't recommend it, as a couple of riders were slightly damaged when it spiraled out of control and crashed into a fencepost. Last year one of my neighbors coated everyone's sleds with no-stick cooking spray. Conveniently enough, she just happened to be participating in the sledding as a spectator sport, but those of us in for a thrill were not disappointed. Do stay on the alert for trees and fences!

4. **Study snowflake patterns**
   Place a piece of black construction paper in the freezer for a while. Take the paper outside and hold it horizontally to catch falling snow. Look at the designs and point them out to your kids. Once inside, make snowflakes out of white paper or coffee filters, imitating the ones you saw outside.

5., 6., 7., 8. **Build snow people, make snow angels, construct an igloo, and instigate a snowball fight**
   These old standbys have a great propensity for lifting spirits.

Finally, when you're pleasantly pooped from the snowy day's activities, serenade yourself with a bubble bath and a few verses of "Let It Snow, Let It Snow, Let It Snow!" You might just wake up in the morning hoping the weather people will begin the day's forecast with "Well, folks, it's not looking good out there . . ."

January 1997

~

Non-literary Nonfiction

I feel as though I've just given birth. An Arts Council grant proposal that I've been nurturing for months—almost nine—is in the mail. I weigh less. I'm walking more lightly. I have a slight sense of accomplishment. And, just as with birthing a child, my overactive ego is whispering about how this contribution to society may benefit the world someday. Still, I'm concerned with how it will turn out. What will the end result of my labor pains yield? The longer I'm away from it, the more worried I become.

So now I'm questioning myself, just as I did as a new mother. Am I qualified enough? Should I even have ventured into this endeavor in the first place? Will I be able to withstand the rigors of being put to the test? Who am I to be playing with such high stakes?

I should probably follow the old adage that no news is good news, yet something keeps haunting me. It's the word *literary.* I submitted my works in the genre of nonfiction, but the Arts Council application booklet clearly states that literary nonfiction is what the judging panel is seeking. I don't know whether I write literary nonfiction or whether my writing is just plain ol' nonfiction. Now, I'm a worried parent.

I turned to my collegiate dictionary for enlightenment and a little consolation, but Mr. Webster couldn't even take the ambiguity out of literary for me. Here's what I found: "1. pertaining to or of the nature of books and writings, esp. those classed as literature. 2. pertaining to authorship; literary style. 3. versed in or acquainted with literature; well-read. 4. engaged in or having the profession of literature or writing. 5. preferring books to actual experience; bookish."

By literary nonfiction, is the committee implying that they want works the caliber of, say, Henry David Thoreau? Or do they merely mean that they won't accept diary entries? And why aren't fiction writers held to the same standards? Does the committee believe that it's not possible to write non-literary fiction, but that non-literary nonfiction is so common they must carefully explain that only literary nonfiction will be accepted? Just as with parenthood, it's all very confusing.

I was in a small, independent bookstore several months ago searching for a certain periodical. I had been told that this magazine was literary. I couldn't find it, so I asked a shopkeeper who appeared knowledgeable and, uh . . . literary, where the literary periodical section was. "I don't know what you mean by literary," she confessed. "We don't have just a literary periodical section. Everything in here is literature."

In a strange way, that woman has given me hope—just as an experienced mother or father can instill confidence in one who is more green at parenting. So I figure that while I may not be very *mothering* in the traditional sense of the word, by the grace (or humor) of God, I am a mother. Though I may not be very *literary*, I have churned out some literature. I pray every day that my babies, and my writing, will turn out okay, and somehow make the world a little bit better, whether or not in the realms of non-literary nonfiction.

February 1999

~

Flowers for My Soul

My father committed to memory and recited many poems while I was growing up. I understood few of the poems, but I loved to hear his deep soothing voice convey the lines penned many generations prior to my birth. Such recitations gave me, as well as the authors and Papa, a sense of timelessness. During those moments I longed for the words Papa spoke to etch themselves in my brain, but they seldom did, or so I thought. Recently because of Papa, a three year old, and some flowers, I grasped some of the significance of Papa's recitations and learned the meaning of Bishop A. Cleveland Coxe's lines in "The Singing of Birds":

> Flowers are words
> Which even a babe may understand.

On a chilly January day, I drove to the grocery store with my three year old and, feeling slightly decadent, picked up some fresh-cut flowers, something I seldom do because they just don't seem practical somehow. Blaise was thrilled with the flowers, although he still wanted a cookie from the bakery. On the way home he asked to hold the flowers, and as I handed them to him, he took them gingerly, as though picking up a newborn chick. Sitting in his car seat, he made up a little song with the colors he cradled: "Pink, white, purple, yellow. . . ." he'd sing and then hum, sing then hum.

When we arrived home it was his nap time, but Blaise was so taken by the flowers that I let him stay up long enough to help me trim them and put them in a jar. He pulled a chair up to the kitchen counter, stood on top of it, and carefully removed the crinkly cellophane. As he separated the stems, he touched and smelled and examined each flower and wanted to know its name. "That's a mum . . . those are carnations . . . that's baby's breath," I told him. He was delighted with the name baby's breath, and placed it in the vase just so. When the earthy clay vase was filled with fuchsias, bright whites, and springtime yellows, Blaise stepped back and grinned admiringly, as though he and God together had created a masterpiece. At that moment I could hear Papa quoting Sadi in "Gulistan":

> If of thy mortal goods thou art bereft,
> And from thy slender store two loaves alone to thee are left,
> Sell one, and with the dole
> Buy hyacinths to feed thy soul.

The magic did not end when we placed the art of God and Blaise on the table. At bedtime as I was singing "This Little Light of Mine," Blaise listened intently to the words. When I finished, he exclaimed, "Mommy, that light is like the flowers we got today!" Blaise, without ever having heard Thomas Hood's words in "I Remember, I Remember," saw with a poet's eye the charisma of our flowers:

> I remember, I remember
> The roses, red and white,
> The Violets, and the lily-cups,
> Those flowers made of light!

March 1999

The Ideal Breakdown

I must attest that some days are indeed better than others. Maybe it was luck or maybe it was the synchronicity of the universe, of which I've been more aware after reading *The Celestine Prophecy*, but either way the gods were smiling on me a couple of weeks ago, and I've been basking in my good fortune since.

The morning began as usual: after breakfast and the hustle and bustle of preparing a one year old and a three year old for preschool, I dropped off the older and then delivered the younger to his school. As I attempted to leave, the clutch slipped when I paused to let a woman walk in front of the car. The car died and wouldn't start again. "Oh great," I thought, "now I'm not gonna get the house cleaned while the boys are in school." Then I realized the silliness in being upset about not having to spend the next two and a half hours sanitizing the litter box, scrubbing the bathrooms, and dusting. I called my garage from the preschool's office. The mechanic I spoke with said that my mechanic wasn't in, but that he should be back in about fifteen minutes. I told the guy on the phone that I was in a bind because my car had broken down and asked if he could please help me.

"Not really," he said. "We take in our own work and I'm a week backed up."

"Okay. Fine," I responded slamming down the receiver.

You may be thinking, "Honey, if that's good luck, I sure don't want any of it." But don't worry, things got better. I bummed a ride to the garage from a sympathetic mother who had just dropped off her child and who said that she couldn't believe how rude the guy who answered the phone at the garage had been. "It's okay," I replied, "they're gonna have to deal with me in person now."

I walked in the garage within five minutes of making my phone call, and there sat my mechanic working on a billing statement. "Hey, honey," he greeted me. I was in no mood for niceties.

"Ken," I said, "my car broke down and I need your help." Ken got up as if his sole purpose for getting out of bed that morning had been to fix my car.

"Well, let's go have a look at it," he said. Ken and I rode in his beat-up old pickup to my broken-down old car at the preschool.

Ken spent about ten minutes assessing the situation and determined that we should get the car to the garage. He said he'd call a tow. My garage, though, just happened to be across the street and a block up from where my car abandoned me, and we were on a hill. I told Ken that I was willing to coast it in if he'd help a little. That's where I recalled the dream I'd had the night before of my car breaking down and my pushing it somewhere. I was by myself in the dream; fortunately I had some help in reality. Ken gave the car a push, and I coasted out of the parking lot, across a busy five-lane intersection, along the road for about one hundred yards, and straight into the garage. "Yahoo!" I called out triumphantly. Ken also seemed pleasantly surprised by our success.

"Hey, we did it," he laughed as he pulled up in his truck. Then commenced the work. Ken spent a solid hour and a half repairing a broken part. When he finished, the car still wouldn't start. He called a buddy who works on imports who informed Ken that the igniter on my car had been recalled by the manufacturer and that I'd have to have the car towed to the dealership.

Ken took me home, I called a tow, then called my husband who picked up the boys from school. After the boys had their lunches and naps, I called the dealer who surprisingly told me the car was all ready to go. When I picked up the car, there was no charge because not only had the dealer paid for the recalled igniter, but the tow as well. Then when I went by to pay Ken, he only charged me for the broken part he'd replaced, not his time. "Since I didn't get the car runnin' for ya," he said.

A car breakdown is always a bummer, but if it were to happen again, I'd want it to be exactly like it was on that day. I broke down during daylight within coasting distance of my garage, met a stranger who was willing to give me a lift, learned that my mechanic cares as much about me as he does my car (maybe even more), experienced efficiency from the tow service and dealership, spent about twenty bucks altogether, and still managed to clear a path through the house. It's not exactly the stuff beer commercials are made of, but some days, and breakdowns, really are better than others.

April 1997

~

The Vitality of a Grave

I like to think of myself as being fair and humane, though my children might sometimes think otherwise; and I like to think that life is pretty much the same—equitable and civilized. The Protestant work ethic and various religious doctrines have imprinted a great percentage of Americans with the notion that if we work hard and do the right things, we'll succeed and somehow be granted immunity from sorrow and grief. While such propaganda can provide the basis for a strong capitalistic society, it doesn't do much for those who seek to make sense of a family member's premature death, or parents who have a disease-stricken child. Though I do believe that lifestyle choices can and do have a bearing on health, disease does not attack a body based on whether one is considered good or bad by mortals.

My husband's brother recently died of various sorts of cancer that had afflicted his body for nearly two years. The situation for Jeff's family epitomizes the old cliché that refers to life not always being fair. My brother-in-law was thirty-eight. He left behind a wife with multiple sclerosis, a ten-year-old daughter, and a thirteen-year-old son. Jeff's death was not unexpected and was, in a sense, a relief because he is no longer in pain. Yet his death left me reeling—smacking me with the fact that my own life is finite, forcing me to look long and hard at post-life existence, and causing me to ask if I am fully living and whether I am passing on to my children the significant stuff of life.

Perhaps in an attempt to find solace during Jeff's funeral and burial, I kept recalling my walk through a graveyard last October. I remembered the beauty, peace, and confidence that I felt in that graveyard. Now, not so much for your enlightenment as for my own healing process, I share some of my thoughts from that day in the graveyard of St. John's Lutheran Church in Charleston, South Carolina.

The graveyard teemed with life on this eighty-degree day. Huge live oaks (so called because they remain green all year round) sheltered birds who busily chattered and worked. Several above-ground tombs were cracked open by years of weathering, allowing me to view the contents—nothing frightening or mysterious—only dirt and small pebbles, as if to emphasize that I will one day return to dust.

Even so, attempts by loved ones to preserve the memory of their deceased were evident in the epitaphs that lingered on some graves, dating back to the early 1700s. I found that heart-broken parents had surely walked this graveyard more than a century ago—two babies from the same family who died at less than two weeks old were laid side by side. Certainly before the days of penicillin, a twenty-two-year-old woman's epitaph indicated that she left behind a young husband to care for her two infant children. Yet an elderly woman, whom the epitaph stated was "doomed to outlive all her children," had finally found solace at this site.

The graveyard seemed complacent and yet full of life, with a young tree sprouting up between two tombstones and older palms shading the plots. Spanish moss danced as a soft breeze rippled through the oaks. An orange cat stared at me indifferently as it lay comfortably on an aboveground tomb as though it were a couch. Here at this place of tombs, I felt the circle of life in a very real sense, and I couldn't keep from thinking whether or not the initial inhabitants would mind sharing their already established burial place with me once I die.

Now Jeff's body lies in a graveyard in Nebraska City, Nebraska, the founding town of Arbor Day. I don't know why he's no longer on earth, and I still want to yell to God that it's not fair. Even so, I know that trees thrive near his vault, that birds play happily over his remains, and that even a cat may one day find a comfortable napping spot on his tomb.

April 1998

Freedom from Violence

This spring's school shootings in Littleton, Colorado, and Conyers, Georgia, have prompted me to think about the term *freedom* and to wonder if Americans need to rethink our love affair with freedom. How free is a society whose children have access to semiautomatic weapons and instructions on how to make bombs? How free are children who are free to play games such as Mortal Combat? How free are the impressionable minds of youngsters who are entertained by acts of brutality on TV? How free are the families of the high schoolers in Colorado who were gunned down while their killers laughed about it? How free are students who must attend school fearing for their lives?

I dare say that when the American Constitution was written, its visionaries never imagined that guns in schools, much less Internet bomb-making instructions, would be points of contention. Surely the authors of the Constitution would be distraught to learn to what extremes the right to bear arms and freedom from censorship have been taken.

My five year old attends school with children who seem to know Jerry Springer intimately, who talk about the short dresses of the Spice Girls, and who play with war toys and video games that make goals of capture, murder, and torture. I've had a very rude awakening, but I still think that most five year olds should be living in the safety of a Sesame Street world.

So I'm frightened, not only for the safety of my own children, but also for the health of my country. If not stopped, the violence and killings will paralyze this nation. Keeping in mind that not all adults should have children in their care, parents, teachers, and adults who do have charge of children and teens *must* set limits. Children function best in a place where their boundaries are established and clear. They should have freedom *within those boundaries*.

Simply put, my children have the freedom to choose between peanut butter and jelly or a turkey sandwich at lunch. They do not have the freedom to pick anything they want. If that were the case, my three year old would have a moon pie, jelly beans, and bubble gum every day for lunch; and what kind of freedom would such a diet bring to his health and teeth?

Some of the most distressing family situations that I'm aware of occur in homes where the children, not the parents, rule. I know of a woman who feels helpless because her teenage son and his friends take over her house on the weekends, toting in guns and doing drugs. Indeed, granting freedom without structure demonstrates a perverse apathy that is likely to lead to destruction in one form or another.

Perhaps one day, America will earn again its envious slogan of "Land of the Free," without the sarcasm that the phrase now implies. In the meantime, I pray to the heavens for saving grace for us all.

June 1999

What I Did on My Summer ~~Vacation~~ Holiday

With summer upon us, I've been pondering how we Americans use our vacation time. My husband Pat always makes it clear that when we're traveling he wants there to be more to our time away than merely vacating. America is the only English-speaking nation, of which I'm aware, in which its inhabitants refer to time off from work or a fun trip away as "vacation." My dictionary tells me that a vacation is: "A period of suspension of regular work, study, or other activity, usually used for rest, recreation, or travel; freedom or release from duty, business, or activity; [and] an act or instance of vacating."

In Australia, Canada, and England people don't take vacations, they go on "holiday." Americans think of a holiday more in terms of a specific event to commemorate or celebrate, such as July Fourth, Christmas, or Thanksgiving. My dictionary includes that traditional definition, but holiday is also expressed as being quite a bit broader. Consider the following meanings: "A religious festival or holy day; A period of exemption from burden: [such as] a holiday from worry; Festive, joyous." Taking a holiday implies that one is savoring the moment so as to become rejuvenated.

I am slowly learning how to take a holiday instead of merely vacating. I got one of my first lessons in holidaying several years ago when Pat and I backpacked through Southeast Asia on a shoestring. On the island of Koh Phangan in Thailand, we stayed on a secluded beach in a bungalow that was built in the top of a tree. I'm not kidding. For two dollars a night we got this small tree hut with a mattress, a mosquito net, a kerosene lamp, and a hammock that hung out front. Our front yard consisted of the beach and the ocean. It was beautiful and simple and we thought we were in heaven. There was no electricity and no hot water, but we could bathe under the palms where there were roofless communal showers that spurted out cool water for an hour each day. There was absolutely nothing to do except sleep, snorkel, savor a good book by the ocean, and eat. No phone; no TV; no going into town except by a lengthy trip on a rickety, over-packed canoe with an outboard motor. Trips into town occurred when one left, not during one's stay. We indeed felt fortunate to have found this little place of paradise and congratulated ourselves on getting into the relaxed and laid-back holiday mind-set. Then one day we realized that we were in grave need of some toilet paper and insect repellant.

Fortunately, there was a small sundry hut on the premises. We visited the shop one morning, but no one was there, and the door was closed. Thinking that we had just hit an off hour, we returned in the afternoon, then again in the evening, then the next morning; but still no one appeared to do business with us. At lunch we asked the owner of the grounds, who was also our waiter and one of the cooks, what the hours of the sundry shop were. He didn't appear surprised, what with us being Americans and all, but he did seem slightly agitated. His eyes narrowed as he focused on us sitting there in our auras of a harried lifestyle that the ocean had not yet washed away. Very deliberately, almost as if it were useless to explain this concept to us, he said, "When he there, it open. When he ain't, it ain't." Pat and I realized at that moment that we were merely on vacation and that we needed to toss our watches and set our bodies and spirits on island time.

Perhaps it was our change in attitude, perhaps luck, but the next day we found a person at the sundry shop. He was lying on a hammock in front of the open door, listening to a boom box, and smoking some herbs that you can't buy at a sundry shop in the United States, at least not legally. He made no effort to get up or move as we approached. We exchanged greetings with the shopkeeper, strolled around the hammock and into the shop, made our selections, walked out, and put some money in his hand—all the while trying to be cool, as if this were the way we normally bought things. The shopkeeper appeared completely unaffected by our being there, having remained in the same position throughout our visit, but he had unknowingly bestowed on us a gift. We walked away from the shop less hurried and a little more present in the moment. We noticed freshly washed clothes hanging in the sun to slowly dry, and just how soothing the songs of the tropical birds were. We returned to our tree house breathing a little deeper and savoring our stay there more intently. We were on island time. And we were on holiday at last.

July 1998

~

Juice, Pooze, and Tattoos

I recently learned something about myself: by no stretch of the imagination am I a businesswoman. Sure, I'm fairly well organized, I'm intelligent, I like working with people, but when it comes to selling stuff in order to make money, I'm a flop. I came to this somewhat unsettling realization surrounded by my hometown folks, an atmosphere that made the facts a little easier to swallow. They let me down gently.

It all started when I agreed to have a kids' tattoo booth at my hometown tomato festival in the Tennessee mountains. I love to watch little kids' faces light up as snakes, rainbows, or cars appear on their bodies. The thought of making money, in addition to what I would make on the tattoos, lured me, so I bought other stuff to try to sell. I bought plastic animals, yo-yo's, tinsel-twirler batons, hair jewelry, bubbles, animal masks, and several dozen jars of something called Pooze, a slime-like substance that makes a poot sound when you stick your thumb in it. Basically, I bought a bunch of junk that I thought kids everywhere would love. Then, as if my sinking a few hundred bucks into cheap plastic toys wasn't enough, I had the fantastic idea of buying individual juice cartons, putting them in a cooler with ice and offering cold juice for fifty cents—something I thought would surely take off, seeing as how the cheapest drink one can get at the festival is a dollar can of Coke.

I came home one evening with nine boxes, each containing ten juice cartons, and told my husband what I was planning on doing. He thought my idea so brilliant that he was certain ninety cartons of juice would not be nearly enough. "I think we should get at least ten more boxes of ten," he told me.

He planned to get the juice the next day, but I met him for lunch and told him that I'd pick up the juice. He forgot. When we came together at the house that evening, I had 50 cartons of juice and Pat had 100. With the previous 90 that I had bought, that brought our grand total to 240 cartons of juice. We were jolly about our mistake, though, congratulating ourselves on the juices that would be such a big hit.

The night before the festival, we set up the tattoo tent, laid out all the toys, and I iced down a good portion of the juice. I made a sign, offering my juice for fifty cents. On the big day, I sold . . . two. *Not* two boxes of ten, mind you, but two individual cartons of juice. My own kids helped themselves to about six of the juices, so at least I got rid of eight. The second day of the festival I got desperate and offered a free juice with purchase to all the customers clamoring at my tent flaps.

So after hours of ordering merchandise, displaying my wares, and working for two days in the hot sun applying tattoos, I'm about sixty bucks in the hole, and have two hundred cartons of juice in my garage. The upside is that the Pooze was extremely popular.

Having my own business has taught me that Pooze and tattoos are assets. Everything else has the potential to put you in the red.

If you happen to be in the market for juice, call me. I'll even throw in one of my few remaining cans of Pooze and give you a tattoo. That's quite a deal, coming from a businesswoman, turned writer.

August 1999

~

Kiss of Death or Touch of Love?

I recently received a call from a friend who began the conversation with, "Oh, Lee Ann, I'm so glad to get you. I'm in a bind and need some help." I thought my friend was probably stranded somewhere and needed a lift. But she continued, "There's a little baby bunny on my sidewalk that's been floundering around for at least fifteen minutes. Its eyes aren't even open yet. I don't know what to do with it. I don't want to touch it, but I hate to leave it there for a cat to get."

Certainly I was concerned about the traumatized bunny. People who only slightly know me know what a big softy I am when it comes to animals. But curiosity, or perhaps ego, got the best of me, and I wondered why on earth Linda would call me—seeing as how my day job is *not* being a veterinarian. There was a brief pause in our conversation while I attempted to sort all of this out. As if reading my mind, Linda said, "I'm calling you because you're a hillbilly and I thought you might know what to do." I was instantly flattered. Of all the qualities that are associated with being a hillbilly, I had never realized that being gifted at animal rehabilitation is one of them.

I immediately dropped what I was doing; grabbed an eyedropper, an old T-shirt, and a shoe box; and went straight to my friend's house. Sure enough, a baby bunny about four inches long lay panting on the sidewalk. I picked it up, snuggled it in the T-shirt, and gave it a few drops of water with the eyedropper. I talked to Linda for a few minutes, put the bunny in the shoe box, and brought it home. My plan was to nurse the bunny through the night and in the morning deliver it to the Nature Center. I called the Carolina Kids' Conservancy, an animal rehabilitation project, to get some advice. The woman I spoke with said that I could feed the bunny a little soy-based formula. "But just know," she warned me as gently as possible, "stranded baby animals seldom survive." Still, I poured myself into rehabilitating the bunny. Before going to bed, I wrapped and rewrapped the bunny in the T-shirt and settled it in the shoe box that I had placed half on and half off a heating pad. At 2:00 AM I got up and fed the bunny some formula, talked to it, and tried to make it comfortable. At 6:30 when I woke up, it was dead.

The death of a baby bunny that I had attempted to nurse through the night was not a good way to begin a Monday. Throughout the day I kept wondering if I had drowned the bunny by giving it too much water, or if the heating pad had been too warm for it. I thought that maybe if I had gotten up again at 4:00 to feed it that it might not have died. How could I be so lazy? I asked myself.

These thoughts played in my head all day, and things seemed only to get worse. I went to the gas station, and after

I filled up the tank, the car wouldn't start. Neither of my kids took naps and were cranky, I got into an argument with my mom, and I kept wondering why I couldn't save a sweet little bunny rabbit.

I didn't realize until my husband came home from work that what I needed was a major shift in perspective. "How was your day?" he asked.

"I've had better," I whined, but I didn't go into details—I had already called him early in the morning to tell him the bunny had died, so he knew about the major incident. There was a pause in our conversation while I busied myself in the kitchen—trying to find something I could do successfully—to take my mind off my defeat.

Pat positioned himself in front of me, looked carefully into my eyes and said thoughtfully, "You know, I've been thinking today that because of you that bunny didn't die without knowing a loving touch."

I had not expected that I had done something beneficial for the bunny, particularly something that anyone else would recognize. I had interpreted the bunny's death as a personal defeat. Pat's insight helped me see past what I thought was my kiss of death to my touch of love.

September 1998

My Treasure

Rather than being with me in the now, in the nitty-gritty work of child rearing, I sometimes feel that the spiritual is more easily discovered in a faraway or mysterious place such as Machu Picchu, a Balinese Hindu temple, a mountaintop, or the white sands of Thailand.

My children have a book that illustrates otherwise. In *The Treasure* by Uri Shulevitz, the poverty-stricken Isaac has a persistent dream that leads him far away from his home in search of a hidden treasure. He does not find the treasure on his journey, nor at his destination—a formidable castle in another city. A guard at the castle laughs at Isaac for following his dream. "You poor fellow," the guard chastises, "what a pity you wore your shoes out for a dream! Listen, if I believed a dream I once had, I would go right now to the city you came from, and I'd look for a treasure under the stove in the house of a fellow named Isaac." Isaac spends several days journeying home and then digs under his stove to find the treasure. He sends the guard a priceless ruby and builds a house of prayer in which he inscribes, "Sometimes one must travel far to discover what is near."

I felt a little like Isaac a few mornings ago, not on a traveling journey and not so cognizant that I was looking for something, but searching nonetheless. Then I found it—not rubies or emeralds or diamonds, as Isaac found—but still something priceless. Here's how it happened:

My six year old, Gabe, has taken a fascination lately with the Titanic. He's checked out a couple of books on the ship from the library. He's not allowed to see the movie that was so popular last summer, but he sat wide-eyed in front of a National Geographic documentary on the Titanic, taking in details that I'm sure didn't register at all with me. Then Gabe said that he planned on drawing a picture of the Titanic and that he needed a *big* piece of paper. I pulled out the colored pencils and a *big* piece of paper. Gabe worked very hard on his Titanic picture—he included its four smokestacks, the iceberg, lifeboats, and distress flares. He was proud of it.

The next morning while he was getting ready for school, Gabe's four-year-old brother came to him looking as if he'd just swallowed a mouse. "I did something, Gabe," Blaise confessed. "I drew on your Titanic picture." Gabe and I both darted to the table and hovered over the drawing. Sure enough, above the ship were red and blue squiggles that formed a circular shape and then fell toward the ship.

I was distraught. "Blaise," I scolded, "you should never mark on anyone's picture, at least not without their permission."

Gabe peered up at me and said, "It's okay, Mom." I waited while Gabe examined the picture of which he'd been so proud. "Look, Blaise," he said gracefully, "I can make your drawing into one of the flares." Blaise, who had thought that he would be reprimanded, opened his eyes wide, and even puffed himself up a little. He had contributed something significant to this Titanic masterpiece.

Gabe could easily have been devastated by Blaise's marks on his drawing. Instead, he turned them into an important contribution, and in the process gave us all an unexpected treasure of acceptance and forgiveness. Most of the time I expect my children to model my behavior. Yet on that day Gabe's example was a shining gift, and I didn't even have to spend days journeying to a castle in a faraway city to find it.

October 1999

~

Picking up the Trash

I am a believer in taking care of the environment, but I sometimes get caught up in the polluted river of buying stuff that I don't need. So last year, as a way of dealing with my hypocrisy, I organized an Adopt-A-Highway cleanup effort. Picking up other people's trash is pretty humbling, but it's also fun socially. Most folks who are willing to wear loud orange vests and oversized work gloves while breathing exhaust and toting huge orange and blue bags along two miles of highway early on a Saturday morning have a great sense of humor.

During one cleanup effort last spring, as I was contributing even more debris to my already heavily laden sack, a man in a car slowed down long enough to make sure that the Styrofoam cup he was tossing out would land squarely in front of us orange-clad cleanup workers. I resisted my first urge to yell obscenities. I even resisted my second urge which was to allow him a glimpse of the middle finger of my right hand. I figured that I'd practice restraint, seeing as how I was with a church group and all. So I fumed inwardly.

A couple of months later, my fellow fashion queens and I were scouring the front grounds of a McDonald's when two young men in an SUV pulled to the side of the road and motioned for me to come toward them. "What are you doing?" the driver asked.

Remembering the Styrofoam cup incident, I feared it might be a trick question, so I answered the obvious. "Cleaning up the highway," I said.

"Are you a convict?" he asked, almost sounding hopeful.

I smiled, but his expression didn't change. "You know, it's funny you asked that," I went on, "because as we were putting on these florescent vests we were saying how grateful we are that they don't have the word "inmate" written across the back."

He gave me a blank look. "So you *are* an inmate?"

"No, no," I confessed, "not yet anyway."

This guy seemed almost disappointed that I wasn't some kind of criminal. "So you're doing this for required community service, right?" he continued.

"Well, it's a community service," I explained, "but it's not required."

"*Really?*" His surprise seemed to outweigh his disappointment of a few moments earlier.

"Yep," I said, "we just do it 'cause we want to."

"Oh wow!" His eyes lit up as if he had just comprehended a new theory in quantum physics. "Well, thank you and keep up the good work!"

He and his buddy drove away smiling, and I found myself happily thinking of them as I bagged whiskey bottles, gum wrappers, soggy hamburger bags, and cigarette butts. The man of a few months earlier who had tossed out the Styrofoam cup right in front of me was long gone.

August 1999

~

A Chinese Thanksgiving

While living and working in China several years ago, I had the honor of meeting a woman named Yu En Mei. Immediately I noted an uncommon serenity and sense of balance. In talking with Dr. Yu and in reading her autobiography, I learned a little about her incredible life, of which I shall give you a glimpse.

In 1951, Dr. Yu was serving a Chinese hospital as chief of obstetrics and gynecology when the Communist Liberation Army took control of her hospital. She was offered a professorship at the army medical school, a post which she readily declined because she did not wish to wear the military uniform required of such a position. She was thus accused of being a counterrevolutionary. That is, she was deemed detrimental to the communist revolution and considered lower than a murderer; and because of her many contacts with westerners, she was suspected of being imperialistic and thought to be a traitor to China.

Dr. Yu was arrested by the Communist Liberation Army and was in prison for twenty-seven years. Eight of those years she spent in solitary confinement in a small underground cell with a mud floor and no light—so dark that she could not see her own hands. The only item in the cell was a bowl with a lid which served as her toilet. She was served the scraps of food from her guards' meals and moldy rice. She was not allowed to walk around her cell, but was made to sit and think about her crime, being able to stretch out and lie down only at night.

Occasionally after interrogations, she was told to write *self-criticisms,* the Chinese term for criticizing your thinking by writing about what you have done wrong. Dr. Yu said that she was grateful for the opportunity to criticize herself because she got out of her cell, saw natural light, could breath fresh air, sit on a high stool at a table, and write.

I am not able here to describe the atrocities which Dr. Yu experienced while in prison. To most of us, though, just thinking about some of the things she was made to do is beyond tolerance. Dr. Yu's youngest brother could not bear the pressures and humiliation of imprisonment, and he committed suicide.

Finally, after her own suicide attempt and horrible betrayals by many who posed as her friends, Dr. Yu was released from prison in 1978. She continued her work in medicine by translating and interpreting western medical journals. Relatives in America tried to persuade Dr. Yu to move to the States, offering her their unconditional support. But she refused. "America does not need me," she replied, "but I can still do something for China." And she did. She worked as an advocate for the education of handicapped and orphaned children. Dr. Yu placed all her funds, including a pension, in a charitable trust for the education and rehabilitation of China's special-needs children.

Of her imprisonment, Dr. Yu says, "I have so much to be thankful for. There is no reason for me to harbor any un-Christian resentment. There is no doubt in my mind that my release—with sanity—is truly a modern miracle."

After living a few months in China, I was grumbling about an apartment with no heat, having hot water only thirty minutes a day, and too much animal fat in the food in the foreigners' compound. Then on a gray, drizzling November day in Sichuan Province, I joined Dr. Yu for Thanksgiving dinner. As we ate tofu soup, fried greens, and steaming bowls of rice, she smiled at me and said, "I just love the concept of the American holiday of Thanksgiving."

Dr. Yu died in 1994 at the age of ninety-one, but her courage, her faith, and her kind and grateful spirit live in many Chinese and non-Chinese whom she touched. Each Thanksgiving I remember our dinner together and am grateful to Dr. Yu for allowing me to glimpse a truly thankful heart.

November 1996

Big Man in a Little Man's Body

"How did such a large man get into such a tiny body?" One of my aunts frequently asked this question, referring to my grandfather who died this year on November fifth. It is a death that has left me to ponder the circle of life more intensely. Though I realize that none of us is immune from death, to me, my grandpa was supposed to be immortal. He'd always been there, quietly grinning and pushing me forward.

I received word of Grandpa's death while on a family vacation in the Grand Canyon. The synchronicity of the universe made itself evident as I recalled how just a few days earlier we hiked into some Anasazi ruins at Mesa Verde. Our Navajo guide, Clyde Bennelly, ventured far beyond mere historical facts and archeological finds to relay some personal customs of the Navajo Nation. Mr. Bennelly told how each person is responsible for touching seven generations: your own generation and the three generations that precede and follow you. In that way, customs and languages are kept alive and one realizes the circle of life. Mr. Bennelly pointed out that when I am born I am in the fetal position and am very dependent. In my old age, I am apt to become dependent for nourishment from children and grandchildren. As I grow older and closer to death, I will likely return to the fetal position that I assumed in the womb and as a newborn. Mr. Bennelly painted a timely picture, because one of the last times I saw my grandpa he was lying on his bed resting peacefully in a fetal position.

Just a few weeks before his death, Grandpa said to me,

"Lee Ann, whenever I've decided I was gonna do something, I've just up and done it. I haven't piddled around. I want to die the same way." And he did. He had been sick with spleen cancer for a while but had taken a turn for the better about a week before he died, and it was congestive heart failure that killed him.

In many ways, Lawrence D. Smith is immortal. He is endeared to many whom he encouraged and listened to as pharmacist and funeral director in my small mountain hometown. He served the community as mayor and Lions Club president. He was responsible for instituting the rescue squad and volunteer fire department. He supported higher education with a passion, serving Carson-Newman College as chairman of the board. He eventually received an honorary doctorate from the college. But in spite of all the titles and civic duties and community honors bestowed on Grandpa, his main focus was encouraging others. Grandpa loved to play the stock market and had made quite a bit of money doing that, but he lived a simple, unextravagant life. He spent his money on the education of his grandkids and others in the community who had the desire but not the resources to go to college.

Though Grandpa was very active in his church, serving as deacon and Sunday school teacher and director for many years, he was open-minded and was not one to preach at or judge others. Grandpa didn't even try to persuade his own children or grandchildren to attend church. He felt that he had set an example by what he himself did, and that if we hadn't picked up on it by watching him then any attempt to persuade us with words was useless. Still he would like to have seen each person in the community in church. One man Grandpa knew was known not to attend church. While my aunts were receiving friends at the funeral home, that man told them that about a week before Grandpa died he had complimented Grandpa on his tie. Grandpa hung the tie around his neck and said, "Then wear it to church sometime."

"You couldn't give me a thousand dollars for that tie now," the man told my aunts.

At Grandpa's funeral my Aunt Bunny told that when she was a little girl she frequently had bad dreams about an imaginary man who lived in the attic—even though she slept downstairs near her parents. When she moved to a bedroom on the second floor of the house, Grandpa came to tuck her in on that first night upstairs. My aunt said that she would have tried consoling her children, convincing them that the man in the attic was merely pretend and that they were safe. But as she phrased it, "Daddy did things differently than most people."

My grandpa, after he tucked her in, said, "Well, you're a lot closer to that man in the attic now." Aunt Bunny said that she never had a nightmare about that man again.

She said, "I knew that my daddy loved me so much that he would never knowingly put me close to anyone or anything that might hurt me, so I must have realized then that the man in the attic was not real."

A couple of months before Grandpa died, my young boys, who consistently gravitated toward Grandpa whenever he was around, started calling him "Greatpaw." His smile at this new name was unmatched. Through my boys, Grandpa reached three generations in the future, and my boys touched three generations back. My sons are two and four, and even if they don't remember Greatpaw, they will have absorbed much of the essence of this "big man in a tiny man's body" that they will pass on to little ones who will one day call them "Greatpaw."

December 1997

Going to School with Bells On

My children have been in school for a few months now. No, they aren't in college, or even high school. But the way people look at me when I tell them that my older son is in kindergarten and my younger one is in a morning preschool program, you'd think my husband had walked out on me for one of the Spice Girls and that the empty nest syndrome is just around the corner. It's as if, after that first day of school, my life became void and empty. "What are you going to do when your boys start to school?" was a question frequently put to me prior to August tenth.

On one such occasion I responded, "Celebrate!"

The inquiring woman laughed in surprise, "Oh, that's not quite the answer I was expecting," she admitted.

Don't get me wrong. I am a doting mother. My boys are an extension of me, and I love them dearly; not necessarily because of the me I see in them, but because of the ways they are so distinctly *not* me—yet still of my blood. I smother my boys in hugs and kisses. I sing goofy songs with them and tickle their ticklish spots. I sprinkle imaginary twinkling star dust on them before they go to sleep at night because they truly believe that Mommy's star dust makes them sparkle. As I was putting Blaise to bed one night he looked up at me and purred, "I love you sweet-honey-baby-angel Mommy." In such moments I get a precious glimpse of the love my boys have been given reflected back to me.

As Kahlil Gibran points out in *The Prophet,* my children are not really my possessions, and their lives have significance outside of mine. They're *supposed* to grow up and go to school. I wouldn't want it any other way. When Blaise started preschool this year he cried—though only for a few minutes—but I didn't. I knew he was in caring, competent hands and that he would learn to adapt to being away from Mommy for three hours. To be quite honest, we all need a break from each other every now and then.

On Gabe's first day of school, many parents lumbered from the kindergarten classrooms with wet cheeks, red noses, and wads of tissues in their hands; but I emerged dry faced. Someone solemnly asked me that same day, "How is Mom handling Gabe going off to school?"

"I think it's fabulous," I chirped. The inquiring person made an attempt to mute her shock and disbelief, and for a moment I felt as if I were being ever-so-slightly cold.

I recalled Gabe's rocky start. He was born more than three months early, weighing about two pounds. His father and I couldn't even hold him during the first month of his life. Once when we were visiting Gabe in the newborn intensive care unit, we watched him struggling with all his might to pull in a breath of air. He turned red then blue, until his monitors alerted the doctors and nurses that something was terribly wrong. A half-dozen neonatal professionals pushed us away from his bedside, and we watched limply, with our hearts in our stomachs, as they aggressively resuscitated Gabe. We thought that we had seen Gabe take his last breath. But with the assistance of the nurses and doctors, and through his own persistence, Gabe pulled in one breath, then another, and another.

This year Gabe started kindergarten—tearlessly. You can bet that if I had a bright pink pantsuit with bells attached, and a hat the shape and color of the sun, and shoes spotted with smiley faces, I would have worn it all on the first day of school.

December 1998

~

Gabe's Star

A few days after Christmas last year I took my son Gabe, who was then two, to a giant toy store to exchange some of the many items which well-meaning relatives had showered on my toddler and his baby brother. The store absolutely overwhelmed me, practically to the point of not being able to function. I felt bombarded by the stuff—all of it toys.

This reaction was similar to how I felt when, upon returning from China, I first entered a grocery store for some popcorn. I was stuck at the beginning of the aisles and couldn't move because there was just too much of everything. There must have been a dozen different kinds of already-popped popcorn but I left the store empty-handed. I have seldom experienced such paralysis. A mental health professional might declare that I was a victim of "reverse culture shock." But if you knew what a popcorn-aholic I am you would think that surely I was on the edge of insanity that day.

In spite of this inability to function at optimum performance when thousands of brightly colored boxes and bags are screaming, "Buy me, no, buy *me*!", I made my way up and down the wide aisles of the toy store. Gabe faithfully held my hand as we viewed the contents of the bulging rows, feeling like foreigners in a place where no one spoke our language. The computer section attempted to seduce us with promises of how intelligent Gabe would become if only I would take one of them home. Gadgets, lights, and horns adorning frightfully real riding toys beckoned with the charm of entering into adulthood. Stacks of videos offered Gabe the prospect of hours of entertainment, and his father and me hours of relief from tending to him. Plastic food items sent an appeal of encouraging a child's imaginative play, but I figured we could use the real thing at home. Gabe expressed interest in several musical instruments. When I explained that I didn't think we needed any more because of the overflowing basket of maracas, tambourines, drums, xylophones, and various other percussion instruments that we already had, Gabe calmly agreed. We didn't even bother with the soldier and gun and war-toy aisle. After an hour in the store, our cart that was nearly the size of a Mack truck housed one bucket of sidewalk chalk, a book, and a Sesame Street barn—and I was very nearly psychotic.

Finally, nearing the cash registers, Gabe picked up a plush Tigger doll that had been pushed under a shelf and was lying on the floor. "Look Mommy," he said brightly, holding it up like a prize.

"Oh, honey," I sighed, dusting some brown dirt off Tigger's leg, "that one's not in a box." A cashier eagerly directed me to the looming display of Tiggers-in-containers so that we could choose a clean fresh-from-the-factory one. "Here, honey, let's get this one," I coaxed, pulling an over-packaged Tigger off the shelf.

"Mommy, Gabe likes this one," he asserted.

I surveyed my unapproachable Tigger in its cumbersome box, paused for a moment and admitted, "I like your Tigger best too, Gabe. Let's get it." The cashier gave us a startled look when I proudly announced that we'd take home the slightly soiled homeless Tigger.

"I suppose that's fine," she said, "but I'll need one in a box for the bar code."

On the way home, feeling that I had been sucked in by an extreme of western capitalism, I fumed silently about all the plastic junk in that one store and wondered why the holidays can't be more simple. Then from the stagnant silence an elated Gabe announced, "Star, Mommy, way up in the sky, a *star!*" I glanced back at my happy two year old clutching what could easily have been a rejected Tigger. Unlike his mommy, he was free to see the world around him because he wasn't dwelling on the stuff in that toy store. Gabe was content with what he held in his arms.

My two year old taught me a valuable lesson that night which I incorporated into my New Year's resolutions. I promised myself that when feeling numbed by materialism and the chaos of consumerism, I would pause, remember Gabe's star, and focus on the simpler things of life. As with most of my resolutions, I cannot claim complete success, but I did eat a lot of popcorn this year.

December 1996

~

Gabriel's Healing Path

For our first baby's delivery, my husband and I had planned a dimly lit room with soothing music. I would practice t'ai chi relaxation techniques interspersed with visits to the whirlpool. When the baby was born, we would celebrate with champagne.

Yet our euphoric birthing wish and my perfectly healthy pregnancy ended when, one week before birthing classes were scheduled to begin, I went into labor for no apparent reason. Gabriel was born at twenty-six weeks gestation, more than three months early, into a hectic room full of medical professionals and ominous, sterile equipment. Considered very, very premature and weighing two pounds, no prognosis was given as to whether our baby would live or die. "We'll have to wait and see," the neonatologists said.

There began a long journey for my husband and me in learning to integrate holistic healing techniques with state-of-the-art medical technology. We studied and implemented Therapeutic Touch, infant massage, and imaging. We solicited prayers from family and friends. We did anything we could think of to help Gabe pull through. Among the respirators, IVs, needles, and surgeries, we wanted Gabe to know gentle skin-to-skin touches, warm voices, comforting songs, in short—love medicine. Finally after three months in the hospital, Gabe came home.

My midwife and doctor insisted that the premature labor and delivery were not my fault, but I frequently wonder if I could have done something differently to prevent all the pain that Gabe must surely have felt due to being born so early. He should have been suckling cozily at my breasts, not hooked up to feeding tubes, respirators, and IVs during his first three months of life.

But Gabe is helping me heal. One evening as we were eating, Gabe asked, "Was I in heaven before I was born?"

"Where do you think you were?" I questioned.

"Oh, I was in heaven with Jesus," Gabe said assuredly.

"What was heaven like?" I asked, wanting to tap into his close connection with the spiritual.

"It was fun," he said simply.

I thought about some of the difficulties that Gabe had experienced in the hospital. "Why do you think you chose to be born to us, instead of staying in heaven?"

Gabe didn't hesitate. "Because I liked you and Papa," he concluded with a smile.

After six years, I felt a powerful, healing light beginning to close the place that still remained torn from his birth. There could not have been anything to make me feel more worthy than Gabe's simple statement of love and acceptance.

Sometimes I still wonder if I could have prevented his early arrival, but my self-deprecation is shrinking like a lone cloud on a sunny summer day. Gabe is healed. I'm on my way, too.

December 1999

~

About the Author

Lee Ann Woods was born Lee Ann Smith and grew up in Rutledge, Tennessee, a rural, one-stop-light town in the heart of the Southern Appalachian Mountains. With a background in English education, Lee Ann has taught English as a Second Language in China and at several community colleges and has worked as a writer for the vice president's office of the University of Virginia.

Currently she is honing her storytelling skills as a children's librarian and is working on her first novel. Her pieces have appeared in various regional and national periodicals and in the book *Chocolate for a Woman's Blessings* (Simon & Schuster, 2001).

Lee Ann lives in Asheville, North Carolina, with her husband Pat and their two sons Gabriel and Blaise. Lee Ann plays the piano and lap dulcimer and takes full advantage of the mountains by hiking, whitewater rafting, and rock climbing with her family. She may be contacted through her website: www.leeannwoods.com.